No More. No Less.

An Artful Cancer Journey.
A Remarkable Community.
A Rediscovered Purpose.

Richard C. Colton Jr.
with Judy Katz

No More. No Less.
An Artful Cancer Journey.
A Remarkable Community.
A Rediscovered Purpose.

Published by New Voices Press
315 West 70th Street, Suite 6C
New York, NY 10023
212-580-8833

Copyright © 2019 by New Voices Press
Published in the United States

All rights reserved. This book may not be reproduced in whole or in part, stored in a retrieval system, or transmitted in any form or by any means electronic, mechanical, or other without written permission from the authors, except by a reviewer, who may quote brief passages in a review. This book is not intended to be used as a basis for any specific medical or other legal decision, and the authors assume no responsibility for any such decisions made in connection with the reading of this book.

Library of Congress Cataloguing-in-Publication Data

No More. No Less.
Published by New Voices Press
ISBN 978-0-9883591-5-4

1. Surviving Cancer   2. Health   3. Diseases and Ailments
4. Melanoma   5. Religion and Spirituality

Cover and interior design by Tony Iatridis, Innovation Design Graphics.

Edited by Kai Flanders, M.F.A. Creative Writing,
Columbia University, 2015.

Copy supervision and art content provided by Taryn Möller Nicoll.

Administrative support, continuity and proofreading by Layla Báez.

Editorial and research assistance by Sherrie Soule and Susan Badeaux.

Cover photo and various interior photographs
by C. S. Grevemberg Photography.

Dedication

*You don't have to be a child to
miss your parents and long for
one more chance to say I love you.*

*This book is dedicated to
my mother Howell Lykes Colton (1915-1992)
and my father Richard C. Colton Sr. (1901-1994)*

No More. No Less.
Is a story of survival

New Orleans philanthropist Richard C. Colton Jr. takes us along on his almost two decades-long battle against a deadly form of cancer, and the spirituality it unearthed inside him. A cascade of treatments plays out over these pages, involving chemotherapy, radiation and three major surgeries. The last operation cost him a radical resection of the left side of his face, altering his appearance forever. With his life hanging in the balance, the author asked for a miracle—and his wish was granted. This is the story of a plea, a promise, and the loving support of a community that gave a man back his life—so he could do more good in the world.

Courage is not the absence of fear, but rather the judgment that something else is more important than fear.

—Ambrose Redmoon

The human spirit is stronger than anything that can happen to it.

— C.C. Scott

We shall draw from the heart of suffering itself the means of inspiration and survival.

— Winston Churchill

Table of Contents

Chapter One: A Shattered Tranquility 1

Chapter Two: Losing a Large Piece of Myself 19

Chapter Three: Chronicling Cancer on Canvas 35

Chapter Four: Leading a Horse to Water 53

Chapter Five: Visible and Invisible Ailments 73

Chapter Six: Do You Know What it Means to
Love New Orleans? 89

Photo Gallery 103

Chapter Seven: A Persistent Adversary, A Continuing
Miracle 121

Chapter Eight: Recovery's Long Road: Becoming
Stronger in the Broken Places 141

Chapter Nine: A Contract With God Fulfilled 161

Interviews with Key Members of My Medical Team
and Friends 179

Acknowledgments 215

About the Author 219

About the Judy Katz 220

1
A Shattered Tranquility
New Orleans: June 2012

Dr. Stephen Metzinger's office was blissfully air-conditioned, a needed respite from the heat that had invaded New Orleans like an unwanted houseguest that day in late June. I was seated on the edge of the examination table, crinkling the sanitary paper. The sound made my skin crawl. I've never liked doctor's offices. I prefer to spend my time at the paddocks with my racehorses, or wandering around an art gallery—or, best of all, conversing with friends over a good meal. At that moment I was wondering how long it would be before I could sit down to a plate of fried catfish at Joey K's Restaurant on Magazine Street. Little did I know I'd have to grow accustomed to hospitals. Their fluorescent lit interiors, overly-sanitized smells, terrible food, and foreboding energy would all too soon become as familiar to me as my cherished local haunts.

I shifted my weight and scratched at the bandage on my neck, which was just behind my left ear. The wound underneath throbbed uncomfortably. Ten days prior, my local ear, nose, and throat doctor, Dr. Burr Ilgenfritz, had lanced what he told me was a boil and then sent me on my way, assuring me that I had nothing to worry about. "Just a little cyst," he had said. Now the site had apparently become infected, sending rays of pain down my neck. Dr. Ilgenfritz sent me to plastic surgeon Dr. Stephen Metzinger for the infected lesion, which had become foul-smelling. He in turn sent me into one of his hospital's surgical suites, where, under local anesthesia, my lesion was washed out with multiple cultures, aerobic, anaerobic, fungal, etc. Many biopsies were taken, and all the cultures came back positive for Staph aureus. As for the biopsies—this was what I was waiting to hear about. Dr. Metzinger had inspected the lesion about a half hour ago, looked concerned, and immediately ordered those biopsies. Now, as he re-entered the examination room, his face was twisted into a grimace.

Stephen Metzinger is a large, athletic man, and from the start impressed me with his professional demeanor. I learned that he had practiced medicine at Johns Hopkins University Hospital, but, forsaking city life, had, to my good fortune, chosen instead to become a country doctor just outside of New Orleans. He said he preferred the slow ebb and flow of life in the South, and liked to watch his kids play sports without having to be constantly paged. I admired that in him. He was a fine doctor.

Today, however, his bright, energetic face had a bit of a shadow crossing it, as though someone had just made an impolite remark at a dinner party. He grabbed a stool and rolled toward me, until his face was even with mine. "How you doing there, Mr. Colton?" he began. He was always friendly and respectful; this time his voice carried an odd tone. From the beginning I insisted he call me Richard, but even now, after so many years, he keeps using my surname.

"Excited to go see the horses run from my usual spot in Saratoga Springs this summer," I said, trying to counteract his somber tone. "You know we don't run them in New Orleans in this heat."

"Mr. Colton," Dr. Metzinger said, his tone becoming formal, "you might need to postpone that trip."

"Why's that? I try to get up there every year."

"I'm going to level with you," Dr. Metzinger continued, pulling his white coat taut at the collar and taking a deep breath. "We got the biopsy results back. What we lanced on your neck isn't a boil. It is a necrotic lymph node."

"What does that mean?"

"I'm sorry to say it indicates what appears to be metastatic squamous cell skin cancer—meaning a form of cancer that unfortunately can be rather aggressive."

The dread words hung in the air like the sour smell of my infected lesion before it was washed out. I had to sit there, stewing in the connotations. Still, something inside told me to remain stoic. This was not a time to panic. This was a time to learn all I could about the enemy.

I had a small amount of experience in the arena. Eleven years before, in 2001, I was referred to dermatologist Dr. Coller Ochsner for a growth on the right side of my forehead. It turned out to be an invasive squamous cell carcinoma, and Dr. Coller Ochsner surgically removed it. One year later, she removed another squamous cell carcinoma on my forehead. I had had a little radiation, visiting local doctors for treatments for one thing or another. None of it seemed out of the ordinary for a man my age, and I was comfortable knowing that my doctors would always keep an eye on things for me. So once again I thought of this new lesion as nothing more than the little medical issues that pop up here and there in life, and are dealt with. Certainly it wasn't anything that was at the forefront of my mind, or had given me concern about my mortality.

Today, I was in shock. How had things gotten so out of hand so fast, despite all these specialists who were continuously monitoring me?

"Okay, the cancer came back and now it's aggressive. Why didn't I know this sooner? Didn't it show up in all of those other tests?" I questioned.

"Your other doctor had ordered a PET CT Scan for metabolically active tumors, and that result was negative. As a result he thought it couldn't possibly be cancer, it had to be a sebaceous cyst. So he lanced it in the office as he normally would, and then packed it, assuming that would be the end of the problem. But he was wrong," Dr. Metzinger said.

Dr. Metzinger pulled his stool closer to me and reached his hand toward my face, his fingers gently coming into contact with my skin. "If I feel just below your cheekbone, I can detect a mass that I believe could be metastatic, which means it spread from your neck. Your lymph nodes have become enlarged, whether by the spread of cancer or by an infection. I can't tell at the moment, but I have to assume the spread is cancerous—until proven otherwise."

My heart pounded in my chest, rising to my throat, which eventually formed words. "Dr. Metzinger, do you think something *will* prove otherwise?"

"Richard," he said, using my given name for the first time, "I can't say without further tests. You need to see my colleague Dr. Paul Spring. He's one of the best oncologists in the area, and he'll be able to perform a thorough biopsy. But in my professional opinion this looks very serious. "

My head swam as Dr. Metzinger slowly explained the details of his preliminary diagnosis and told me my next steps. Thankfully, he had it all written down for me, since in my shocked state I was not retaining much of the information. I thanked him and left the room in a daze. His receptionist tried to speak to me on the way out, but her words sounded like they were coming from someplace deep underwater.

I staggered out into the street. The extreme heat outside was something I could technically feel but didn't fully register. Vaguely, I thought I should cover my exposed skin from the hot sun. I've always had a fair complexion and burn easily. Then I thought: "Well I already have cancer, so what use is it anyway?"

It wasn't until I got into my car and started the engine that my thoughts snapped back into clarity. I understood that I was facing down something serious, something I might have to go to war against, but in truth I didn't yet fear for my life. If it turned out that I needed surgery I would have it, and everything would be fine. Life would go back to normal, I told myself.

I didn't want anything to mess with my normal. Of course, normal in New Orleans isn't what most people imagine when they think of normal, and my life also was not "normal" in the 9 to 5 sense. At this stage I was a most fortunate man. My life was filled with art and music. With long lunches at restaurants where every waitress knew my name. With long nights spent under the porch-light gabbing about anything and everything with fascinating friends like Judge Dennis Waldron. My normal was pretty damn good, and I wasn't prepared for it to be disrupted. New Orleans folks can be suspicious of outsiders, and here was cancer, more than an outsider—it was an interloper: an interloper I could not simply say "be gone" and then show it the door.

As I drove down the Pontchartrain Expressway, zipping

by the Mercedes-Benz Superdome, I reflected on how my life in this city was something I had created and now longed to continue indefinitely. Though I wasn't born here, my family had established a prominent shipping business in the ports of the Mississippi River, and I had come down after college to participate in the business. Over the course of five decades I had indeed established a life here. I wasn't ready by a long shot to give all that up. I had to finish what I had started in the Crescent City.

Pulling off the Expressway, I parked directly in front of my house in the Garden District, urgently needing the comfort of my home. My house is a columned manor, large and well kept, but not ostentatious. Its manicured lawn and drooping trees fit in with the surroundings—streets lined with other historic mansions. Evenings I like to sit on my porch and listen to the sound of cicadas rising in the trees, or sit in my parlor watching a Yankees game while sipping a diet Coke. It's a large house for a single man, but it's usually occupied by a visiting friend or two who keep me company.

When I opened my door this day I was as always greeted by my enormous portrait of Fats Domino, which dominates the entry hall. My house is filled with art. There are paintings of horses parading the grounds of famous race tracks, medieval art depicting the Virgin Mary, simple portraits of people working in kitchens or workers laying down floorboards. There are also massive sculptures in my front yard by various local sculptors. Inside, with not enough room on my walls to hang the artwork I've accumulated, there are canvases all over waiting to be hung, most wrapped in butcher paper. I've always had a huge interest in the arts, especially paintings. To me, a life without art isn't worth living.

Maybe that's the New Orleanian in me talking. But after the day I just had with Dr. Metzinger not even Fats Domino's smiling face could cheer me up. My future seemed to be cut short, definitely promising pain. I knew cancer was something people *could* beat, something people *did* recover from, but this diagnosis seemed so new, and so severe. I didn't yet know much about my particular form of the disease, and clearly had a lot to learn, but that dread word "metastatic" was certainly not one anybody ever wants to hear.

I decided to remain optimistic. Perhaps Dr. Spring's biopsy would be negative. Maybe this would all just be a minor blip on the radar—a good story to laugh about at my table at Joey K's. Yet later, as I lay in bed that night, unable to sleep, something in my gut told me otherwise.

***

New Orleans: July 2012

It was cancer and it *was* metastatic. Only about a month later I underwent my first oncologic surgery. The summer was still smoldering on, the heat a boiling point that made stepping outside feel like entering a sauna. Dr. Paul Spring, the local oncologist recommended by Dr. Metzinger, performed what he described as "a parotidectomy and lymph node neck dissection." That's doctor talk. In plain English it means that he removed forty-four lymph nodes from my neck and face.

Unfortunately, I've had to become quite adept at doctor talk. It helps to understand the language that dictates your survival. I also understood, beneath the medical jargon, that my chances for survival were less than optimal. A few days after the procedure Dr. Spring called me, and, as kindly as he could, delivered just about the worst news anyone can hear. He told me that a total of seven of those forty-four lymph nodes tested positive for metastatic squamous cell skin cancer. To survive I would have to immediately start chemotherapy—which, as it turned, out, lasted for just two sessions. It didn't work for me, since the drug they used, Erbitux, caused discomfort and rashes. What followed was another series of radiation treatments. Of course when he gave me that news Dr. Spring didn't talk about survival and say that my life was on the line. He didn't have to—I sure got the message.

I was at home when I got this news, and immediately I called Dr. Metzinger. I believe he had known I was in serious trouble from the first moment he saw my neck and felt the mass inside my cheek. Now, with the facts laid out scientifically, he could be completely frank with me. That didn't make any of this easier to face, but there we were.

"It's stage four metastatic cancer," he had to tell me. "It doesn't get much more advanced than this. It's going to spread fast."

"How fast?"

"Fast enough that I think you should start to get your affairs in order."

Get my affairs in order. The phrase dropped on my psyche like a ton of bricks. Suddenly my mortality—my looming death—seemed real. While I wasn't young by any stretch of the imagination, death had always seemed like something intangible and far away, as I imagine it does for most of us— at least while we are healthy. Now it was something I could reach out and touch. All I had to do was put my hand on my neck or my fingers on my face.

"You mean like a Will?" I managed. "I already have one, but I guess I should update it."

"I think that would be in your best interests."

What would be in my best interests would be to survive! I thought to myself, but held my tongue. "Thank you, doctor."

"You take care of yourself, Richard. I'll see you soon."

I hung up the phone. Sitting alone in my living room, surrounded by my paintings, I felt the acute sting of being told to "get my affairs in order." But when a doctor tells you to do something like that, you do it. Those words had hit hard. The doctor's directive forced me to mentally examine the life I had built for myself. Being born into a wealthy family like mine comes with certain complications; it isn't always easy to know people's motives. Whatever the reason, though I've had plenty of girlfriends, I never married. So here I was, a lifelong bachelor, seventy years old, with no heirs. My widespread family didn't need my money—they had their own. I was at a loss for what to do with all of my considerable assets.

I decided to call my friend, business associate, and cousin-in-law Bronson Thayer and get his advice. Bronson had been diagnosed with pancreatic cancer a few years back and was now getting treated at the MD Anderson Cancer Center in Texas, fighting his own hard battle against the disease. Like me, he could afford the best care, but he was subject to a greater reality: the reality of the disease. It was a phrase I would still have to get used to. A lot of new words and phrases were going to enter my lexicon—none of them welcome additions to my vocabulary.

Bronson lived down in Tampa, Florida, and was married to my cousin Stella. They too were a sporting couple. Like me, she owned racehorses, and we met every year at the

Harvard-Dartmouth football game. Bronson had gone to Harvard, and, as for Dartmouth, my heart belongs to the school because my father went there. I grew up in the northeast, and often went up to Dartmouth to tailgate the games. Bronson and I bet each other on the game every year, maybe twenty dollars. Whenever we talked the conversation would start there. I'd say something like "Maybe you should give me points because Dartmouth hasn't beaten Harvard in four or five years." That never worked. We were just like two kids sitting in a clubhouse, joking and having a good time.

Bronson picked up my call on the first ring. His jocular voice sung through the line, immediately lifting my spirits. "Hey Dick, how are you this fine afternoon? Better than your sorry excuse for a football team, I surely hope."

"I have a question for you: how many Harvard men does it take to screw in a light bulb?"

"Oh you son of a...."

"One. He holds the bulb and the world revolves around him!"

Bronson's laughter sounded through the receiver for a moment, then was interrupted by a fit of coughing. "Sorry about that, Dick," he said. "Seems that my delightful disease has spread to my bones. My doctors are scratching their heads or maybe scratching their asses, I can't tell. But never mind that. You didn't call me to talk about cancer."

"Actually," I said. "I did."

"How's that?"

I proceeded to explain to Bronson about the last two months of my life. I went over Metzinger's diagnosis and his mandate that I should "get my affairs in order." It felt good to tell someone, and not be totally alone with this monumental information. Just speaking the word "cancer" aloud to someone other than a doctor felt oddly liberating, as though by articulating the word I was robbing it of some of its terrible power.

Bronson listened patiently, only speaking after I had run out of breath. "That's good advice," he said finally. "To get your affairs in order."

"Are *you* really that resigned to dying?" I asked.

"The hell I am. I'm going to wrestle it down until my last breath. Getting your affairs in order isn't just about figuring out what will happen to your money or your things after you die. It's about figuring out what you want to do with the precious time you have left. Cancer is a funny thing—it's an opportunity just as much as it is an obstacle. It puts things into sharp focus, like a pressure cooker for life. It forces you to make decisions in the here and now, because you know you're headed to the by and by."

"So I've got more to think about; more than just my Will?"

"Your Will is important, but that will sort itself out. What your charge is now, besides finding the best doctors and treatments that you can, is to meditate on how you want to spend the time you have left. We all die; some of us are just dying faster than others. That means we have to live at a more purposeful speed."

"I've always been someone who's gone at my own pace," I replied. "I've done good things with my life…"

"But still, have you done the things you were truly put here to do?" Bronson interjected.

"I'm not sure I know what that is."

"Well," Bronson said. "It is now truly the time to figure that out, and then to hop to it. You have the resources, you have the smarts, and now you have the motivation."

"Thank you, Bronson," I told him. "You're the first person I've opened up to about this. It takes a load off my mind."

"No problem," he said, switching from his almost sermon-like tone to a more conversational Southerly manner. "Any decent ponies in that beat-up lot of yours?"

"I think I have one that might be a winner at Saratoga Springs this year. Shame I won't get to see him run. I have to start chemo that week."

"Ah, the fun part," Bronson replied.

"Thanks again for the kind words."

"You take care of yourself, Richard. And get busy *living*."

I called Bronson to speak again many times over the next few months. I had started with just two sessions of chemotherapy; when I had a truly bad reaction and it was clear the chemotherapy would not work on me, the doctor prescribed a regimen of massive doses of radiation. Over the course of this regimen those conversations with Bronson were a great help and he and I became very, very close. That is one thing about cancer: it will definitely make you closer to people that you know also have it. It's a club to which no one wants to belong.

To be honest, I didn't come up with an immediate answer to the challenge Bronson posed to "live more fully in the here and now." In those early days of my disease I didn't fully comprehend the battle I was facing. Sure, I was more markedly aware of how valuable my time was, but I was still searching for the legacy I wanted to leave. I was, however, determined to not just sit around in a funk, so I did go to the New Orleans Fair Grounds Racetrack often that autumn. It's not as fine a track as Saratoga, but I rented a box and invited friends to join me. Judge Dennis Waldron and his sons James, Matthew and Andrew, usually dined with me afterward. These were not somber meals with an elephant in the room—they had all became close confidants, so they knew my situation and we even joked a bit about it. We also had long, serious talks about spirituality and God. That topic had always been a part of my life, but lately, for obvious reasons, it had leapt to the forefront of my mind.

On those fall days, I liked watching the horses go around and around the track. To me it seemed a potent metaphor for human life. We too will often run in a circle, panting and sweating, urged on by an invisible whip. Once in a while we can break free of the pack, and emerge victorious, having reached our true potential. I knew it was my time to break away. I just needed to fill my lungs with air, set my resolve, and push forward. Meantime, the radiation treatments seemed to be working, in that they were keeping the disease at bay. They were no walk in the park, but tolerable. At least for now.

In April of 2013, I also went for daily sessions in a hyperbaric chamber over a period of several weeks, hoping that the excess oxygen would help promote healing. Did it? Your guess is as good as mine. I was just giving myself every possible edge.

* * *

New Orleans: May 2013

Eleven months after I was first made aware of my extreme cancer status, I got a phone call that would further alter the course of my life. An art broker I had known for years called to tell me that a promising young artist named Taryn Möller

Nicoll had just moved to New Orleans and was looking to meet people in the art world.

"Of course, invite her to meet me for lunch at Commander's. Always happy to meet and encourage young talent."

Commander's Palace is a wonderful old restaurant in the Garden District, just down the road from my house and across the road from the famous cemetery where Lieutenant William Clark is buried. The restaurant is named for this former governor of the Missouri Territory who led the historic Lewis and Clark expedition and helped broker the Louisiana Purchase. Some say Commander's is the best restaurant in town. In a town like New Orleans, with so many fine restaurants, the subject is highly contested, as you might imagine.

Entering the central dining area I spotted Taryn immediately—a slender young woman in her mid-twenties, seated at my usual booth. She stood up as I walked over, and offered me a handshake.

"Nice to meet you, Mr. Colton," she said. "I've heard a lot about your contributions to New Orleans art."

I detected an accent and she explained that her family was from South Africa. Because of the political turmoil there, they had emigrated to the United States. She really came to life when discussing her art. "My artwork is largely biological and biographical," she told me, as I cut into a slice of pecan-crusted fish.

The word "biological" piqued my interest. "How do you mean *biological*?" I asked. "Is it scientific?"

"Yes, but perhaps not in the way you'd think," she replied. "I'm fascinated by the intersection of fine art, medical science and the human body. The vast array of things that accompany these journeys, like x-rays, ultrasounds, CAT/PET scans, microscopic internal photographs, extracted plates and screws, are all fascinating to me."

My fork paused halfway to my mouth. "I can't believe you're saying this to me," I replied.

"Sorry, why's that?" she said, puzzled.

"Those are all the things that are filling up my life at the moment. You see, I have cancer."

Perhaps not surprisingly, Taryn didn't react to the word the way most people do. She didn't fall all over herself apologizing for the disease. She treated me as a "person *with* cancer" rather than a cancer patient. "I'm actually going to be having major surgery in the near future," I reported, as a spread of rich desserts were set on the table. "I just got the news that my radiation isn't working out the way that the doctors were hoping it would."

"I'm sorry to hear that," she replied, taking a bite of cheesecake. "It's funny that we should meet under these circumstances."

"Serendipitous perhaps."

"I don't know if anything is serendipitous when it comes to cancer."

"No," I said. "But maybe when it comes to art."

"We'll have to keep the conversation going then. You can stop by the gallery and see some of the paintings I'm working on."

"I'd like that," I said, and motioned for the restaurant's wandering jazz group to come over to our table and play us a song.

After dessert I helped Taryn into a cab and headed out into the balmy evening. We had spoken for so long that it was now dusk—the lamps along the avenue were clicking on, drawing fleets of gnats and mosquitoes. It was that special time, which filmmakers call "The Magic Hour," when it is still light but there are no shadows. It felt like both the beginning and the end of something. My body felt imbued with purpose.

After meeting Taryn, I immediately checked out some of her paintings on my iPhone. I thought her work seemed vital—something that could really make a difference in the world. Her passion rubbed off on me. I wanted to not only help her in her artistic journey, but be a part of it. I could always cut an artist a check, as I had many times before. This time however, I wanted the partnership to be something personal and purpose-filled. As I drove the few blocks back to my house, I began to connect the dots in my mind.

I resolved that, given Taryn's gift for medical illustrations and her "biological and biographical" bent, this could become an artistic connection that would illustrate my cancer journey. In addition to my role as a collector or patron of the arts, at this juncture my own body could be part of the process. I suddenly decided that I would ask Taryn to chronicle my cancer through her art, and do it in a way that might help others. I was also going to reach out to the God I had rediscovered later in life, when I converted to Catholicism. This conversion had been largely thanks to my friendship with a beloved figure in New Orleans, the late Father Val McInnes, whom I had lost as a friend and mentor several years back, and whose presence I felt in my darkest hours.

That night, home in bed, I surprised myself and did something I had never done before: I made a contract with God. Speaking to Him directly, not just in my mind but out loud—living alone has some advantages—I said, "I have more projects I would like to do. Please help me through this and I'll pay it back a thousand-fold with good deeds. As long as you keep me alive, I'll keep doing good in the world every way I can, without seeking credit. This I vow to you."

Instantly a sense of peace settled over me. That night I felt a new strength enter me: strength I would need, going forward. I had no idea what was coming, and in truth nothing could have prepared me for how much of myself I would lose along the way, how unrecognizable my exterior appearance would become. But with God on my side, along with my team of fine doctors, and Taryn's art as well, perhaps my cancer journey would not be unbearable. Perhaps my life could continue on this admittedly narrow and bumpy road for many more years to come. That was my hope.

In an unexpected way I had begun to "set my affairs in order."

* * *

18 No More. No Less.

2

Losing a Large Piece of Myself
Baltimore, Maryland—September 2014

Looking out the window of the cab, I watched the Patapsco River whip by. Its waters looked cooler and grayer than the muddied flow of the Mississippi. I was filled with a sense of apprehension that deep, dark bodies of water can instill in a soul. It makes you feel as if you are unmoored, drifting out into the unknown, ready to sink down into mysterious depths from which you may never emerge. Or maybe it was just my state of mind, having recently been diagnosed with stage four metastatic squamous cell skin cancer that likewise threatened to sink me into mysterious depths.

The cab hit a bump. Jolted out of my morbid daydream, I felt a steadying hand on my shoulder. Dr. Rebecca Metzinger, an eye surgeon and Dr. Stephen Metzinger's wife, was riding with me. My cousin John Carrere was also in the cab. He pointed out, at a cluster of freighters chugging through Baltimore's harbor. "Look, Dick," he said. "Our old friends!"

Preoccupied with my thoughts, I hadn't noticed them. Now I took stock of the behemoth shapes, pushing through the current like advancing glaciers. These ships were more modern than the vessels John and I worked on in New Orleans all those years back. After both John and I had graduated from college, we ended up working out of the same office. After many years of working together in the steamship business, we had called it quits around the same time. Now we enjoyed a weekly lunch together at Joey K's. He was a member of the reserved table at which we held court.

It was John who had introduced me to horseracing. He had a classmate whose family ran a small breeding operation in Shelbyville, Kentucky. Little by little I began dabbling in the horse business. I would buy a racehorse, pair it with a good trainer, and then see if it had any traction at the track. Sometimes they did. I have a lot of fond memories of John and me watching one of my Shelbyville horses stomp across a finish line.

Today was a more solemn occasion, and I was very glad John was once again by my side. We were in Baltimore, heading to dinner to meet with the noted surgeon Dr. Anthony Tufaro. Dr. Tufaro was set to perform surgery on me the next day at Johns Hopkins. Rebecca had organized the dinner.

In the two years since Dr. Metzinger's stage four diagnosis, my cancer had continued to spread, as stage four cancers tend to do. To stem the tide, I had had a series of procedures done by local surgeons in New Orleans. Nonetheless, an invading army of cancer cells can be held back for just so long. Now it was time to call in the big guns—the General, if you will. Tufaro was recognized as top brass in the field. I sure hoped his skill would do the trick for me. That's why we set out for Johns Hopkins, where Dr. Tufaro was going to surgically remove some large invasive tumors in an effort to stem the advancing tide for good.

I was happy to have Rebecca there as well. She had acted as a protector in many ways during the early days of my treatment. When I underwent radiation, she was very careful to make sure that they didn't give me any more than they should, and made a shield that would cover my eye, which was my good eye. My right eye was damaged by a small stroke some years ago, and I could only make out vague shapes with that orb.

John was still staring out at the steamships. "You ever miss working on them?"

"Sometimes," I replied. "Not much. I miss the track more."

"We'll get back out there again," John said, reassuringly. "All of us together. Now let's go see what this Yankee doctor has to say."

"Let's just pray he's not a Raven's fan," I quipped.

"Let's just pray he prays."

Chuckling, I paid the cab and the three of us stepped into the Charleston, a fine restaurant in Baltimore. Thankfully, as it turned out, Dr. Tufaro was not only a man who prayed, but a man I immediately trusted. He was one of those men in possession of a robust calm demeanor and can command a room without dominating it. That's a rare quality to find in someone, as is loyalty, or the ability to tell a blue joke without having it seem offensive. When you encounter those kinds of people in life you do well to add them to your circle.

Adding people into my life was an unforeseen upshot of this cancer process. Before my diagnosis I had thought that my circle, if not closed, was pretty much complete. But now, as a mechanism of survival, I had to interact with a whole host of new people, most of whom I would have never encountered had I remained healthy. I was building a new community of health professionals, a vital team I was coming to rely on more and more.

From the moment the four of us broke bread together, Dr. Tufaro became a vital member of that community. As we ate, he told us about his journey in the medical field. "I went to dental school initially," he reported, buttering a piece of bread. "I was board certified as an oral and maxillofacial surgeon, and practiced as an oral surgeon and maxillofacial surgeon for about six years."

"What made you go back and start medical school?" John inquired. I kept quiet, mesmerized by Dr. Tufaro's fingers manipulating the butter knife. Those same hands would be cutting into me tomorrow, wielding any number of instruments a thousand times more dangerous than a dull butter spreader. I tried to study them for any sign of tremble, any flicker of uncertainty. I could find none.

"I wanted the challenge. I wanted to do more," Tufaro was saying. "I came to Johns Hopkins after graduating from medical school, and did a few years of general surgery before training there as a plastic surgeon. Then I went to the Memorial Sloan Kettering Cancer Center in New York City for a one-year post-residency training fellowship in the Department of Surgical Oncology's Division of Head and Neck Surgery. That was from July 1997 to July 1998."

"Sounds like you are prepared for a lot of challenges," John commented. "Well," Tufaro said, "I like to say that surgically I can wear two hats. One is as a reconstructive surgeon, the other as a surgical oncologist, removing tumors. Sometimes I wear one hat, sometimes I wear both hats."

"You might have to wear three hats with me," I interjected.

Dr. Tufaro laughed, and I noticed even when his body shook his hands remained steady. "I'll have to wear a lot of hats in your surgery," he agreed. He stopped laughing and became serious. "Mr. Colton, I have no intention of being excessively optimistic about your procedure, or its aftermath. I'm a surgeon, which means I'm a realist. I have to be."

"Richard isn't in the business of being sugarcoated," Rebecca interjected.

"If I was interested in that we wouldn't be here, we'd still be back in New Orleans," I agreed. "The waitresses are pretty there, and if they don't remember your name they just call you 'Handsome.'"

"Here they just call me doctor," Tufaro replied. And then, finally using my given name as urged, he got down to brass tacks, so to speak. "Richard, as you know, by the time you got to me your cancer has progressed to the point where the left side of your face was paralyzed. The tumor had moved from the side of your face into lymph nodes in the gland right in front of your ear, and destroyed the facial nerve, which is a problem," he said.

After silently absorbing all this for a few moments, I asked: "How big of a problem?"

"The facial nerve is the one that animates your face. The problem is that once the tumor has proven to be aggressive enough to metastasize—to leave its primary site and go into lymph nodes and invade something like a nerve—that tells you about the biology of that individual tumor. The truth is that a large number of people get skin cancers that are superficial. You get a lesion on your forehead, the dermatologist takes care of it, and that's the end of it. When you came to me your disease was already pretty far along."

"Are you saying, if I'm hearing you correctly, that Richard might lose a large part of his jaw? That this surgery could make a difference in his face?" John asked.

"I'm saying it's a possibility. I don't know how damaged that nerve is. But we have a strategy in mind, something to offset the potential loss of tissue."

"Is this where the other doctor comes in?" I questioned, aware that a second surgeon would be participating, but not sure exactly what he would be doing.

"Correct," said Tufaro. "My partner Dr. Cooney, who is also a plastic surgeon, and specializes in reconstructive microsurgery, will be there for the reconstructive portion of the operation. The plan is for him to take a piece of tissue, with the artery and vein that supply that tissue, from your forearm, and use it to fill in any gap. This is called a 'free tissue transfer.' We take skin that had been on your arm, with a vein and artery attached. We attach that to an artery and vein in the neck. In other words we are putting a piece of your own living tissue in there. The body will accept what's its own. If it was from someone else it would reject it."

"In truth this sounds pretty gruesome," I had to admit. "Do I have a choice?"

"Not really," Tufaro replied. "You do however have the choice to trust me."

"Not too much of a choice, but I'll trust you anyway."

"Good," Dr. Tufaro replied. "If you can do that I think we'll have more than a doctor-patient relationship. I often get emotionally involved with my patients. I take this all personally. I'm proud to say I've had family members come to me and tell me what it meant to their loved ones." I take this all personally."

"Hearing that means a great deal to us," John said. "Down in New Orleans the personal relationship is more important than anything else. If you don't have respect and a personal connection you don't have anything."

"Listen," said Dr. Tufaro, leaning forward in his chair. "I had this one very famous patient I treated. I can't say who, but I'm happy to say that he's still alive. After the surgery he invited me to dinner with his family. "You know how many doctors I have met in my life?" he asked me. I said I had no idea. He said: "Dozens. You know how many doctors I have invited to sit down for dinner with me and my family?'"

Dr. Tufaro held up his fingers to form a zero.

"He said he didn't know why he liked me, but he did," Tufaro continued. "The bond patients feel is special, and reciprocated, because I feel it too." He sipped his water and went on. "I do have experience treating patients that a lot of other people do not want to treat. I am well trained to do it. But a lot of surgeons, particularly cancer surgeons, unfortunately come off as aloof when dealing with patients whose life may end during the course of their treatments. I say if they feel you truly care about them as a person that will make a huge difference to all concerned. And I do truly care about you, Mr. Colton; okay, *Richard*."

"Can you make me one promise then?"

"Depends on what it is."

"Don't let my life end tomorrow." I held my breath.

"While I can't promise what you'll look like or what your future will hold, I'm not going to let you die on that table tomorrow. I can tell you that, quite frankly."

"Good enough for me."

After dinner we all shook hands and parted ways. From this point on I would have to go without any more food or drink. Surgery was scheduled for first thing in the morning. Now I needed some sleep, as did Tufaro. Back at the hotel, Rebecca gave me a big hug and John gave me a warm handshake before he headed up to his room. He didn't say much, but the look in his eyes gave me the reassurance I needed. I would not be alone.

That's one thing I like about Southern men—we respect each other. John had the same measured demeanor he had when my friends and I talked and ate around the table at Joey K's. He didn't over exaggerate the moment, he just let it breathe. I went into my room, trying to stay calm and focused for whatever lay ahead.

***

Dawn came quickly, light spilling into my hotel room like sugar from a spoon. As I dressed and washed up, it occurred to me that this might be the last time I would get to shave the face I had called my own these past seventy-odd years. Drawing the razor across my cheeks, I took stock of myself in the mirror. The chemo and radiation had reddened my skin, which was also spotted with masses of scar tissue—but it was still my face. It had changed over the years—from age alone—but was still what I expected to see when I looked in the mirror. It was who I was, at least in a cosmetic sense. This could be the last time I would get to see this version of myself. I wondered if I would recognize myself after the surgery, and what impact that might have on my psyche.

I toweled off, took a deep breath, and headed downstairs. John and Taryn were waiting for me in the lobby. I was glad Taryn, who was not able to join us for dinner, had made it there this morning. Over the last two years our artistic relationship and new friendship had deepened. She had gotten to know me as a person, and had become an integral part of the new healthcare community sprouting up around me. In fact, it hadn't taken long after our first meeting at Commander's Palace for her to begin accompanying me to doctors' visits and radiation sessions. Her artist's mind was so curious, always wanting to learn more about every medical process. She was fascinated by all aspects of it, down to the specific names of the tools used and methods employed by my surgeons.

It also had not taken long for us to come up with a specific creative project. We mutually decided that with the doctors' permission Taryn would be in the operating rooms and sit in on my surgeries. The purpose was for her to use them as inspirations for her canvases. Those oil paintings that would result would not be limited to simple depictions of the procedures. Ideally, they would be emotionally evocative experiences that communicated all the pain, vibrancy and danger of late-stage cancer treatment.

By this time—my third surgery—she had already sat in on two previous surgeries, and finished a painting based on them that she titled, "Monoplace: A Portrait in Recovery," which we had unveiled at my birthday party the previous year.

"The hardest thing for me today," she told me, as the three of us drove to Johns Hopkins, "will be suspending emotion. The heart will always quickly overtake the mind if you let it. I have to go into it with a clinical eye."

"Sometimes you can't stop yourself from feeling," I said.

"What are you feeling right now, Richard?" she asked.

"Like I wish we were driving to the race track," I said, trying to lighten the mood.

"Aw c'mon," John said, doing his best to do the same. "You know they don't run the ponies this early in the morning."

We checked in at the front desk. Shortly thereafter I was left alone in a small room to undress, and then moved into another room to be prepped for surgery. I hated the way I looked and felt in the hospital gown, with its ugly green color and open back. Trying not to think about what was coming next I dutifully stretched out on the gurney and waited for the nurses. They came in a few minutes later: two talkative, brassy women who wasted no time in wheeling me into the operating room. "How you doing, Honey?" one of them asked me.

"Honey. Mmm, okay," I joked with the nurse. "Is that a Baltimore expression or do you really like me?" I asked. I always like to joke around with my nurses and waitresses. It helps me get to know them, and often we form a friendship. However, this time it was not meant to be.

"It is a Baltimore thing," the other nurse replied dryly. When we reached the operating room, my initial thought was that the operating table was much smaller than I'd ever seen. I didn't know how I would fit on it.

As I was helped up onto the table, I noticed that the nurses wore lanyards along their necks with Baltimore Ravens insignia on them. "This can't be happening," I said aloud. "I'm a diehard Saints fan from New Orleans being prepped by Baltimore Ravens fans!"

My joke clearly didn't go over, since they immediately put the anesthesia mask on me, and told me to count backwards from one hundred. If you've ever had general anesthesia you will understand how remarkable it is to go out like a light, usually by time you count to ten, and when you wake up it seems like a moment since they first put the mask on. It's especially amazing to me, since, as I later learned, my complicated operation, with two surgeons, a team of nurses and anesthesiologists, and Taryn's sitting in with her camera to capture every aspect of the operation as well, turned out to be a grueling thirteen hours long.

* * *

When I opened my eyes it was just color and voices. Where was I? Who were these voices? Faintly, I identified John. He was on the phone talking to his wife. I could hear them speaking of everyday matters; he was unaware that I was awake. I tried to move and found that I could not. The same with speech. I was conscious but unable to interact with the world around me. My vision, never great, was totally blurry, as if I were at the bottom of a pool. But the voices of John and his wife were clear, and a great comfort to me as I lay immobilized. Then I fell back into a deep sleep.

When I woke up again, it was dark. I could move slightly, and turned my head. When I looked down I saw John sleeping on the floor next to my bed because he didn't want to leave my side. The true extent of his affection and loyalty didn't sink in until later. He didn't have to talk, or even wake up: his presence just provided me with a sense of assuagement in this time of pain and confusion. I went back to sleep yet again, eased back into slumber by the powerful anesthetic still coursing through my veins.

The next time I awoke, Dr. Tufaro was standing over my bed. The nurses, lanyards still dangling from their necks, were changing my IV, and it was painful. That's one thing I hate about hospitals: someone is always waking you up to stick a needle in your arm.

"How long was I out?" I asked. "Did the Saints win the Super Bowl?"

The nurses rolled their eyes at me and flitted out of the room. Tufaro chuckled and checked my chart. "Actually you've been in various states of 'out' for almost twenty-four hours," he reported.

"How did it go?"

"The surgery was successful, but difficult. It was a thirteen hour surgery, Richard. Nobody was expecting it to be that intense."

"So you had to remove a lot of tissue?"

"I don't want you to talk too much now, but, yes there was significant removal of the facial mass."

"Oh," I said, feeling a dead weight rising from my stomach to my chest. This was not sounding so good.

"The first time we change the dressings, I want you to be ready," he said. "We'll do it together, but it might be tough." When I was well rested, Tufaro took the dressings off, and I was able to get a look at myself. I was more astonished than disheartened. My face was still very swollen, but I could tell that a large portion of my jawline had been removed. My eyes were puffy, and the skin around my jaw was raw. It was difficult to see myself so diminished—that was not my familiar face staring back at me. I just didn't look like the idea of Richard that I held in my mind. Which is to say nothing of my arm. It looked like something out of a horror movie, since, in order to heal, the wound had to be kept partially open. I hated to look at it, and it hurt like hell. I felt like some sort of science experiment: parts of me were being used to keep other parts functioning.

However, I am an optimist by nature, and a realist. I knew I would have to change my feelings about my new face. My old appearance was never coming back, but I could build a new sense of self—one based on the community of artists, friends and supporters of all stripes accompanying me on this journey. I hoped that would be enough to compensate for and "fill in" the pieces of myself that cancer had taken.

I'll admit I was nervous, that first time, to look at my altered self in the mirror. I had to keep reminding myself that what was done was done. I'm a firm believer in accepting what life throws at you; you cannot change it. Otherwise you'll be spending all your time worrying about what *might* happen, instead of facing what *has* happened. Still, it's not easy to see what's missing, and different, and not feel like some sort of freak. I allowed myself to wallow in self pity for about an hour, and then gave myself a good lecture. "The fine doctors—and God—have just saved your life, Dick; man up. You were never that handsome anyway," I told myself, and laughed out loud. Good to know that my sense of humor, at least, was still intact.

* * *

After a few days in the recovery room I was moved into my own room and allowed more frequent visitors. Aside from John and Rebecca, Taryn was one of the first to come see me. She bounded into the drab room, full of energy, and drew a chair up to my bedside.

"How are you feeling?" she asked, concern edging at the corners of her eyes.

"Not too bad," I said. "Just tired and my arm hurts like hell. I guess seeing my face isn't a shock to you. You saw it removed."

"It's a part of who you are now. Your appearance does not shock me," she said matter-of-factly.

"Did you see the whole surgery?" I asked.

"Of course."

"Tell me everything about it," I said.

"Are you sure you want to know?" she asked.

"How many people get to relive their own surgery?"

"It lasted a full thirteen hours. I was so fascinated. I'm

sorry: is that a strange thing to say?"

"Not at all."

"I know I am supposed to be clinical, and I was, but the human component was the most interesting part to me," she replied. "The first thing you notice is how the surgeons are almost like gods, holding life in their hands."

"You were standing right on the floor with them?"

"In full scrubs, the whole deal. I even had an approved camera for taking pictures. First, they prepared you: got you situated perfectly on the table, sanitized all their instruments, and cleaned the skin around where they would make the first incision. Right before they made the first cut, Dr. Tufaro stopped everyone and they did the 'Time Out' procedure. He called *Time Out* in a commanding voice, and the twenty or so people in the room all froze. He actually gave your personal background before they began to operate on you. He told everyone your age, mentioned that you were from New Orleans, an art lover, a real Southern gentleman. Someone very special whom he cared about."

Hearing this, my heart swelled. The fact that Dr. Tufaro had taken the time to humanize me, at the exact moment when I was most vulnerable, meant the world to me. Tufaro had given the other doctors and nurses an idea of my identity. I wasn't just a number: I was an actual person they were working to save.

I found out later that this practice isn't common anymore. Nowadays, to cover themselves legally, the surgeon usually just reads the time and the patient's name. Knowing this further deepened my respect for Dr. Tufaro, who had taken the time to revive the ritual for me. "The emotion of the moment was rather overwhelming," Taryn continued. "When they got started I was right in the middle of the action, peering over Dr. Tufaro's shoulder, between him and his assistant surgeon. I was snapping as many photos as I could. It was this tremendous balancing act: I had to hover as close as I could, but be sure not to touch the surgeons."

"Incredible," I mouthed.

"Dr. Tufaro was so helpful. He would even let me know when it was a good time to take certain photos. He knew you really cared about it. It was almost like a master class. I'll show you the photos once we have them processed."

"I can't wait to see them."

"I can't wait to get started on this painting," Taryn said.

I resolved to heal as quickly as possible so that I could stand beside her when it was finished and show it to the world, or to whatever interested parties there might be. Together we would transform pain into meaning, and disease into art. I would just have to learn to live a new kind of life with a partial face.

* * *

34 No More. No Less.

3

Chronicling Cancer on Canvas
Baltimore, September 2015

The Johns Hopkins' William H. Welch Medical Library has the proper regal decor common to hospital and university libraries. Walking slowly along creaky mahogany floors, my gaze turned upward to scan rows of painted portraits of stern-looking hospital officials. "A fine tradition in every medical school," I could imagine Taryn saying with a little laugh. Well, I thought, today Taryn and I are going to inject a little life into that fine tradition. Today we start a new tradition of our own.

We had come to Baltimore to unveil Taryn's latest painting to a crowd of friends, doctors, and, of course, the requisite hospital officials. Titled *Time Out: Tufaro, Cooney and Colton*, the large oil on canvas is a stunning visual representation of my thirteen-hour surgery with Dr. Tufaro and Dr. Cooney. I was amused that it took a man with cancer to liven up the hospital's art collection. But then again, my life is filled with oddities.

The unveiling was held in the library's main reading room. I watched as people began to trickle in. Of course John was there, smiling, sipping a drink. I also watched with joy as one of my best friends, Ernie Carrere, who had spent most of his life as a monk, came through the door. He had flown all the way to Baltimore just for this event, and I hadn't been sure he would be able to make it, but the look on his face when he saw me told me I never had anything to worry about.

"Never ones to reunite under normal circumstances, are we?" he quipped, giving me a hug.

"Ernie, I don't think there's much of anything in my life these days that you could consider normal."

"Dick, I don't think there ever was," he joked. "And that's the way we like it."

"Well, stay tuned for later," I said, pointing at the veiled canvas in the middle of the room. Ernie winked at me, and went off to talk to Dr. Tufaro.

My good friend Joe Wick came with his wife Ginger. Joe, who has since passed away, suffered from a blood disease, and was also being treated by Dr. Tufaro. I saw that Dr. Cooney, the second surgeon in my operation, had arrived with his wife, who worked as a researcher at the hospital. Dr. Cooney had done a world-class job of using a skin graft from my arm for my face.

The event hadn't begun, but I was already feeling the unique sense of community that lovers of art have when they gather. People from all parts of my life, from all walks of this earth, had come together to see the painting. To some it might just look like oils slathered on a piece of canvas; to me, when viewed in context, it was so much more.

After shaking a dozen hands, I wandered over to Taryn, standing near the draped artwork, a smile on her face as Dr. Tufaro introduced her to all the "important" people in the room. I stood by her side as she told, and retold, the story of how the painting had come about, with me interjecting comments when I had something humorous or pithy to add. Here is the story from my perspective:

The previous September, shortly after I left the care of Dr. Tufaro and his team, Taryn began work on the aforementioned painting that would become "Time-Out." Her intent was to create an artistic document that would express our shared vision of my journey, with all its intensities and realities. The finished canvas would communicate our shared philosophy on the challenges and community my cancer had created. There would be a focus on the doctor/patient relationship, along with a visceral depiction of the patient's body. We agreed on these elements, and I told Taryn that I wanted her to have total artistic freedom with the piece. I only asked her to include color, movement, and detail. I saw these motifs as endemic to my experience, and she agreed.

Over the next few months I would get a fascinating glimpse into her process. Meanwhile, my ongoing treatments, although grueling, were going as well as they could. It was completion of this painting that helped keep my spirits up. Some deep part of me was thrilled, in an almost childlike way, to be the main subject of something so beautiful, so potent, and ultimately so life-affirming.

Now the painting would make a transition from artist's studio to the real world. As the group gathered closer, Dr. Andrew Lee, Division Chief of Plastic Surgery at Johns Hopkins, came to the front of the room and, holding a crystal goblet, hit it with a small spoon. In the ensuing silence he gave a short welcome and introduction, relating many of the facts I have just told you. Then he called me over to also welcome everyone and make some remarks about the painting: what it meant, and especially what it meant to *me*.

To this day I have no recollection of what I said. My mind is funny that way. I can remember some things clearly, but often large events, things I *should* remember, are lost in the haze of time. Fortunately I have good friends who remember things for me. I recently asked John what I said. He told me that I had spoken simply, giving thanks to Dr. Tufaro and the whole team at Johns Hopkins, to Taryn, and to all my friends and supporters who had shown up. That sounds about right. I certainly *was* feeling grateful that day, not only to the team of doctors, but to everyone in my life.

Then it was time. Taryn came up, said a few quick words, and together she and I pulled the sheet from the canvas. I can tell you it had to be one of the most electric moments that this sterile hospital library had ever experienced. I will say *Time Out* is unique. The first thing you notice is how large it is. The painting, shining in its gold frame, towered over my head, and I'm over six feet tall. The second thing you notice is the color: red, orange, and blue jump out at you like July fireworks over the Mississippi. Next the forms, the people, begin to take shape. Two doctors in scrubs, my own face, a section of my skin, my jaw—all exposed. *Time Out* is a painting that has a lot of life and blood to it. It's not gory, but you can see what was actually going on during my surgery. Some people have said it made them uneasy. Most said they were totally entranced.

While I had of course seen the painting before this official unveiling, this moment brought it into a new context. Frankly, I was emotional. For me, Taryn's art had accomplished what I thought was beyond possible, even beyond belief. It was a crucial part of the new life that faced me. I was starting to feel what was going on in my cancer battle in ways I had never felt before. Those feelings intensified when Dr. Tufaro came up to speak. I had not known that he was going to say anything to the crowd, so the fact that he stood beside me in front of Taryn's painting was remarkable. Here was the man to whom I had been as vulnerable as one could be, literally under his knife, and here we were, together, celebrating that vulnerability in a totally new context.

Immediately commanding the room in a way that only the most accomplished, steady men can, Dr. Tufaro began: "What really hits home for me about a painting like this is that it reminds you of how much the work we physicians do means to the patient and to their loved ones. If we as surgeons ever lose touch and don't remember that, we would need to stop working. If we ever forget how much our work means, we should no longer be doctors."

His sincerity and warmth were evident, and he beamed as the crowd broke into applause. I looked around again at the stern portraits above us: we were certainly injecting some spice into these hallowed halls.

When the clapping died down, Tufaro continued: "This painting is a great portrayal of why we do what we do. Now Johns Hopkins will have a constant visual reminder of that duty." He paused, and then his usually stoic demeanor took on a softer expression. "By sharing this painting with us, Richard is actually sharing an important part of his life. His experience, as depicted here, no longer belongs to him alone: it is now a part of all of us. Richard will always be a significant part of my story as well. Not only as a patient, but as someone who challenged me as a surgeon. Someone I worked very hard for. And someone whom I know and respect as a man. We know each other well. Being his doctor has been a true privilege."

I'm glad Dr. Tufaro was looking at the audience and not

directly at me as he spoke, because there were tears in my eyes. Always able to read a room, Tufaro then lightened the mood. "And by the way, if you think the *surgery* is well portrayed, that's nothing compared to how accurately my cap and scrubs were painted!" Among laughs, he concluded, "Truly, Taryn and Richard, we are all amazed by this work, and are delighted to have it in the Johns Hopkins family!"

As Tufaro stepped away to thunderous applause, I had to quickly regain my composure, since Taryn and I had a little trick up our sleeves. She took the microphone, and motioned for me to join her. "Instead of myself or Richard talking about the details of the painting to all of you, we have a little surprise," she said, and then handed me the microphone.

Here I do remember what I said. "Well, nothing about this ceremony is conventional. The painting certainly isn't, so we're going to present it unconventionally. We're going to ask the doctors themselves to identify which portions of the surgery were represented, to give you a feeling of the painting from the medical perspective. And also so I can learn exactly what happened to me on the operating table!"

Some nervous laughter followed. We had taken both the audience and the doctors off guard, but our gamble paid off. Dr. Tufaro and Dr. Cooney went through the whole canvas, identifying key stages of each procedure and what body parts were involved. In other words, they gave us an intensive medical tour of the whole piece. In doing so they brilliantly shared what I had gone through, enlightening everyone as to what they were seeing in the painting. I myself was rapt the entire time. This was my body on display, being described to me in detail. I was mesmerized, and clearly so was everyone else. As the two surgeons spoke you could have heard a pin drop.

As the program wound down, people came up to me to say how moved they had been, and assembled doctors commented on how refreshing it was to see something so bold and colorful in this space. Ernie told me it was now one of his favorite paintings, up there with some portraits of saints that he loved. "I'm more of a New Orleans Saint than a saint, saint," I told him. Taryn was practically glowing as she shook hands and took compliments. She deserved every one.

I did overhear some people say that they thought the painting was somber. When they looked at it, they said, it brought up their own mortality. They weren't prepared to have that effect when looking at artwork. Clearly they didn't want to think about what could happen to them or a loved one. While I understand their reticence, I have never, and would never, think of either Taryn's painting or my cancer journey as somber. For me, *Time Out* was something progressive and triumphant, and represented our journey. The very title *Time Out* is a way to humanize the patient before he or she is cut into. In this case it was Dr. Tufaro, as I said earlier, who had taken a few precious moments before the surgery to call attention to me as a person.

To me this painting inherently humanized me, making my struggle real and tangible. How could that ever be thought of as somber? Cancer may be a difficult topic, and perhaps my attitude can be seen as atypical. I do try to stay positive, but realistic, addressing whatever comes up head-on. Many people want to run from the topic, pretending it doesn't exist. I simply have no time for that. I can't turn away from cancer. I certainly can't turn away from the reality of *my* situation, and wouldn't want to even if I could.

Later, I discovered that *Time Out* had been unveiled directly in front of a painting of the four founders of Johns Hopkins, painted by the renowned portrait artist John Singer Sargent. Those were the stern men I had been looking up at during the ceremony. I may have been a bit too critical of their portraits, as there was, and still is in some places, a "fine tradition" of such paintings. Looking back, I find it immensely interesting, as a patient, that the people who founded the school were watching over the doctors currently serving the institution.

Nonetheless, I must say, respectfully, that I like Taryn's painting quite a bit better then these portraits. They represent very different eras: history and modernity existing side by side. Another example of such a juxtaposition might be the architect I.M. Pei's ultramodern glass pyramid, which was built in front of the classic facade of the Louvre Museum in Paris. Well, nobody is better than a couple of honorary New Orleanians, Taryn and me, to usher in the new, the exciting, and the colorful.

That is how *Time Out* found its permanent home in the plastic surgeons' conference room at Johns Hopkins. The idea was for it to be seen by people who are passionate about the subject, who can identify the procedures taking place, and who might even recognize some of their fellow surgeons. This room is a much better spot for it than a public walkway. I don't think we could have given it a better home.

* * *

New Orleans, December 2015

December is a calm month in New Orleans. Mardi Gras mania will not begin until February, and the oppressive heat of summer has lifted for a while. People usually take time off work for the holidays to visit with family, or to simply enjoy themselves. We're good at enjoying ourselves down here. We've practically made an art form out of it.

So that's what I was doing the day I got Dr. Tufaro's call—enjoying myself. That included a long lunch at Joey K's, the famous eatery and my favorite lunch place, where I shared my usual reserved table with Judge Dennis Waldron and his sons. We had talked about the influx of young people currently flooding into the city. We were in agreement that they didn't bother us, as they did some people, and that we didn't expect that any significant number of them would stay long enough to become New Orleanians. We also agreed that you had to have been born here to be a true New Orleanian.

"Well, except *you* Richard," said Judge Waldron. "You're an *honorary* New Orleanian."

"Appreciate that."

"Don't mention it."

Back home, I was thinking about that conversation as I sat and contemplated my beloved artwork I like to surround myself with. Then the phone rang. I never answer the phone myself. One of my nurses—they had all started staying longer hours at the house after my surgery—picked it up. "It's Dr. Tufaro," the nurse said, coming into the sitting room with the cordless.

Dr. Tufaro? What could he be calling about? I had seen him just a few days ago after I'd gotten some routine scans done. Up to that point everything seemed to be progressing just fine, which is to say that the cancer was *not* progressing. I took the phone, my hands a little less steady than they had been a moment before.

"Richard Colton here."

"Hi Richard. How are you doing?"

"Yankees are winning, so I'm okay. To what do I owe the honor, doctor?"

"Well Richard—those scans we did last week have come back. They turned up some unexpected results. I'll just come out and say it. The tumor we originally removed has grown back aggressively."

"Has it now?" I asked automatically, for the moment not really taking in what he was saying. On the television screen I watched Derek Jeter hit a home run. Or was it a fly ball? I couldn't tell. I felt as though I was underwater, drowning. Coming back to my senses, I realized Tufaro was still speaking. "It's at the point where it was almost the same width as the original tumor. We can't deny that the rate of growth is pretty alarming. Whatever cancer cells were left in your body quickly mutated. Even if there was only one cancerous cell left after the ones we removed, what was left was apparently enough for the tumor to regrow."

I felt myself slowly coming up for air, my faculties returning. I had been through this before; I knew what to do. Namely, ask questions. Get to the point. "'What does that mean for the immediate future?" I asked, trying to keep my voice steady.

"The fact that it has returned, and completely regrown within a year after our last operation, is not encouraging," Dr. Tufaro replied. "The cancer is definitely not yet under control."

Well, that's quite an understatement, I thought. At that moment I was more frustrated and disappointed than actively frightened. Truth is, at the time of the *Time Out* painting's unveiling I had believed, or wanted to believe, that I was out of the woods. Or, if not completely healed, at least on the path towards being cancer-free. For months after that long surgery all my blood work and treatments had been good. Now, looking back, I realized that this new tumor must have already been growing inside me, even on the day of the unveiling. Had I known, how different my mood might have been, and how differently that day might have gone. I'm glad I didn't know.

"I'm thinking I'm going to need to book a ticket to Baltimore," I said.

"I want you back in surgery within two weeks," Dr. Tufaro said.

So that was that. Right back where I started. I can think of no circumstance that more dramatically highlights the duality of my situation than this one. No sooner had I finished creating art and finding love within my community of friends and doctors, then I was thrust back into the uncertainty of my needing another serious medical procedure. That's the real kicker with cancer: how it can, in a matter of seconds, make every part of your life subject to a catastrophic shift. One moment you're sailing along, having lunch with friends, or watching the Yankees. The next you're slated to be sliced open again. For some, and that includes me, it is simply the nature of this cancer beast.

* * *

A little over a week later I was back at the restaurant in the Baltimore Four Seasons Hotel, having dinner with Dr. Tufaro, John, and Taryn. Cousin John was sipping his signature drink, an "Old Fashioned." It was close to Christmas. When we had arrived at the hotel earlier that day we saw how beautifully decorated everything was, and how everyone was in high spirits. It was all happiness and joy. My little group and I, however, were in a far less festive mood. Everyone else was celebrating, and we were praying to God that the surgery tomorrow was going to finally finish off the cancer. It was ironic to be surrounded by such positive external stimuli, which contrasted so dramatically with what was going on in my life.

Breaking bread with my surgeon before a major operation was becoming something of a Richard Colton tradition. I wondered how many more of these dinners I would have to have. Hopefully, not too many more! Or maybe, I told myself, it *was* better that there be many more: that there would never be a "last supper," so to speak.

That night, for some reason, I was confident that this would *not* be my last supper. I remembered how, the night before my first major surgery, Dr. Tufaro had promised me I would not die on the operating table. His reassurance had given me great comfort: nobody wants to die on the operating table. Or wants to die, period. As I sat at the table, and later, back amongst the splendor of the hotel, his words echoed in my mind, calming me. A remarkably gifted doctor such as Dr. Tufaro promising to at least get you through to the next step in your journey is definitely a sentiment that stays with you for a very long time.

I thought of Tufaro's words "I won't let you die on the operating table" as my second contract. The first, again, had been with God. This one was with Tufaro. Though he probably wouldn't describe it in this manner, I felt I had entered into some sort of universal agreement that would keep me alive. He just had to do his part, and I would do mine.

It was the same with Taryn: I also had a spiritual contract

with her that kept me going. As long as she was turning my struggle into art I had to be there for her, to provide her with material and support. Aside from the fact that we grew to become close friends, part of the reason she was here with me in Baltimore was to observe my surgery at close range—right beside the doctors in the operating room—and again turn it into art. I had no intention of stopping our project before it was finished.

I now had contracts with God, with my surgeon, and with my artist. With each person I was entrusting a different part of my life. With God I was entrusting my life's purpose. With Tufaro I was entrusting my physical well-being. With Taryn I was entrusting the artistic portrayal of my cancer journey. In each "contract" there was a spiritual, physical, and mental component that helped me believe in my continuing survival. The next morning I was wheeled into surgery; again they made me count back from one hundred under the hands of questionable Ravens' fans, and again I went under the knife. Once again—no surprise—Dr. Tufaro kept his promise, and I did not die on the operating table. I awakened in the now familiar Recovery Room, foggy and confused. John was by my side, and let me know that the world had gone on turning while I was out.

* * *

Given the circumstances, the surgery went as well as it could have gone. This operation, at only five and a half hours, was much shorter than the first time. However, it was getting increasingly difficult for Tufaro—or any doctors—to operate on me. Chemo had not worked, and I had already reached a lifetime maximum of radiation. Those procedures, over time, bleach the targeted tissues. As a result, when surgeons are looking at a surgery site they have to continuously double-check every time, using a nerve stimulator, to see if they are cutting muscle or nerve tissue. As they cut deeper and deeper into the parts of my tissues that had been radiated, it becomes much more challenging for them.

As soon as medically allowed Taryn came to visit me. From her I learned what had happened while I was under the anesthesia. She also had amazing photos from the surgery. I have to repeat: It is such a rare thing, getting to *see* what happened while you slept.

"Richard, you look great," she said, pulling up a chair.

"Liar," I said.

"What did you call me?"

We laughed, and she began telling me about the surgery. "Dr. Tufaro's surgical partner was this young, really hip blonde woman. She had Christmas earrings dangling down from her ears. When she handled surgical equipment you could see she had her nails painted Christmassy colors. It was a very soothing environment in the operating room."

"That's good," I said.

"The surgery went smoothly, and took about half as long as last time. When it was over Dr. Tufaro came out, and he and I sat with John in the little waiting room. It was very late at night. John was reading his financial newspapers."

"Always," I laughed.

"Dr. Tufaro didn't elaborate on your surgery, and John didn't pry him with questions, which was smart. Basically we were all winding down from the intensity, and just made small talk for a good half hour, comparing Christmas plans. Dr. Tufaro told us that the Royal Family of Saudi Arabia was flying him out over the holiday to perform surgery on one of their loved ones. We were heading home to New Orleans and he was being flown to Saudi Arabia! That was kind of surreal."

"Like a strange dream."

"I do remember the mood of our conversation changing a bit at that point." Taryn continued. "He was definitely concerned for you. The fact that the tumor had come back in such a short amount of time was upsetting. At the same time, Dr. Tufaro seemed confident in the work he had done. He was very honest with us and said we needed to be on guard; that this was not something that was going to go away without an important fight."

"Nothing goes away without a fight."

"Don't we know it!"

"Did you get enough material for another painting?"

Taryn patted my hand gently. "Of course I did. And I can't wait for you to see it."

"I'll make sure that I do."

After Taryn, I had a much less welcome visitor: The Goon Squad. That's my nickname for Dr. Tufaro's residents, who were tasked with handling the daily hospital rounds. They came through every morning, and several more times throughout the day. They treat you like a case number. They wake you up at 5:00am and expect you to be ready to talk. They gave me information while I was still under the influence of medication, hardly awake. Anybody who has ever spent any time in a hospital is familiar with their own Goon Squads. It wasn't Dr. Tufaro's fault. It was simply a reality of hospital life and is part of every surgery. Maybe I am being harsh with what I named them, but for one thing I really hate having my blood drawn before breakfast. I'd like to imagine you may feel exactly the same.

That night a massive storm whipped through Baltimore. So much rain poured down from the heavens that the windows began to rattle and shake. I got a little spooked and called an attendant to the room. I wanted to know what kind of practices they had in place if the power went out. Bottom line: I wanted to know what they were going to do to ensure *my* safety. The attendant didn't have much to say. He didn't seem the least bit worried about it.

"Send in a nurse please," I requested firmly.

"Fine," he said.

The nurse came in: an Asian man I had never seen before. He looked as unconcerned as the attendant.

"What if the power cuts off?" I asked.

"If something goes wrong we have codes."

"What kind of codes?"

"We roll you down the steps to somewhere else. Somewhere safe."

"Is there anybody else that can help me?" I asked.

"I'm the only one here. It's the middle of the night."

"What would *you* do under those circumstances?" I asked. "What would *you* do if you were stuck here without power?"

He smiled and said, "Oh, I'll be just fine. My wife picks me up every evening at 11:30 and takes me home, so I don't have anything to worry about. I'd just wait until 11:30."

I had to laugh. What else could I do? Sometimes hospital life is so ridiculous you have to capitulate to the absurdity of it all.

"You'll be fine too, sir," said the nurse reassuringly as he left the room. Outside, the rain kept pounding on my window.

***

Toward the end of my stay at Johns Hopkins, Dr. Tufaro undid my dressings, then handed me a mirror from the bedside table, and allowed me to see my face. Now that the swelling had gone down I could clearly see that I had lost much more tissue than before. In fact, the entire left side of my face was sunken in—any semblance of a jawline there was gone. I had grown used to looking different, but this was far more dramatic. Now even more of my face was gone, perhaps never to return. "Metzinger can fix a lot of it," Dr. Tufaro said. "As a plastic and reconstructive surgeon he's a wizard with this stuff. You'll have scarring of course, but it can look a lot..." he struggled to find the words.

"Better?" I asked.

"I didn't mean..."

Suddenly, a phrase ran through my mind: *I am what I am: no more, no less.* In that moment I realized I was still the person I was before the surgery. That saying could be invoked anywhere and be true. *I am what I am: no more, no less.* Why did I need to try to reconstruct myself to be the person I used to be, when I could just be satisfied—even proud, as a survivor—to be the person I was now?

"I am what I am. No more, no less," I told Dr. Tufaro.

"Damn right, Richard."

"Of course I want to do whatever you think might help me *medically*. But I don't think I'll want any plastic surgery," I said. "Not to restore my handsome face," I said jokingly, though we both knew I was dead serious. "I think I'll wear this new face of mine as a badge of honor."

Dr. Tufaro smiled and shook my hand. This decision may seem strange to many people. For most people losing almost half their face would most likely be their biggest issue. In a relatively short time it has become a non-issue for me. I look in the mirror and, yes I see what others see. And, in truth, what some look away from—though thankfully never anyone in my inner circle. I really do wear my new face as a badge of honor. It is a visible token of what I have survived on my cancer journey. I'm not hiding from that.

One of the nastiest things about cancer is that it comes from your own cells. What invades you isn't a foreign growth from out of nowhere. This dread disease attacks the body parts you've had your whole life, including in my case the tissues in my face and the bones of my jaw, and then turns them against you, an enemy within. I like to look at it as this: every part of my face that has changed is a sign of me not letting cancer win. My new profile is also a conversation starter when I meet another cancer survivor. We can identify each other and have an instant bond. When you're in a battle with cancer that immediate rapport and sense of unity is important for anyone.

Incidentally, Taryn made another remarkable painting based on this second surgery. That painting now hangs in Dr. Tufaro's office. I can't think of a better place for it.

***

4
Leading A Horse To Water
New Orleans: July 2016

I had just finished checking the baseball scores—my Yankees had, thankfully, beaten the Orioles with a walk-off homer—when the doorbell chimed. My pulse quickened with the hope that it was Matthew Waldron. That would mean it was now time for us to leave for Saratoga Springs, New York, which was even better news than The Bronx Bombers latest win.

Susan, my nurse, went to answer the door, rolling my suitcase behind her. "I think I know who that might be," she said in her Louisiana drawl, which was quite a bit thicker than my own. Susan is my main nurse and takes excellent care of me. She came into my life about a year back, just after my second extensive surgery at Johns Hopkins, and quickly became a key element in my daily routine, what with an endless bevy of pills to swallow, tests to run, and medical appointments to attend.

After two major surgeries in as many years, I needed assistance. Working with Susan has developed into a wonderful partnership, one that continues to this day. Right after she began working with me, it became apparent that she understood my sense of humor and—this is important—likes eating at Joey K's just as much as I do. Well, perhaps not *just* as much—I don't think *anyone* likes eating there quite as much as me.

Susan was not the only member of my new healthcare crew: I had other nurses and aides who came at night. What my medical team worried about most was the possibility of my falling, so having someone capable there with me at all times was critical. Prevention is the better part of valor after all.

Susan opened the door and, sure enough, there stood Matthew, his lean and steely build housed in his usual outfit of a polo shirt tucked into khaki shorts. Come to think of it, that's what I was wearing too: it's something of a uniform for Southern men in the summertime.

"Good morning, Richard," Matthew said, taking my bag from Susan like a gentleman. He turned to me, smiling, pure resolve and spry energy. "You excited to get out there and get on with it?" he asked, pointing over his shoulder towards the car.

"Oh you betcha Matty," I replied. It was time to hit the road, and he would be a fine companion. I had met Matthew in 2004 at—where else but Joey K's! Like others, I immediately gravitated toward his intense positive energy. A year later I invited him up to Saratoga, and he's been a staple of the upstate New York trips ever since. We've actually traveled all over the United States together and attended the Kentucky Derby together three times. What I value most about our friendship is that we are the type of guys who go to ball games even when there's hardly anyone else in the stands, just for the love of it. It could be a Yankee game or a high school playoff game, it doesn't matter to us. Sometimes we have more fun at the junior games. One time a kid collapsed on the court with a cramp and we watched in amazement as they raced out with *pickle juice* for him to drink, which immediately resolved the issue!

Matthew is the athletic director at Stuart Hall For Boys in New Orleans. His motivational attitude toward life has always elevated my mood. During times when my illness got me down, or when I was caught up in the general lethargy of life, Matthew buoyed my mood, helping to keep me "on track" as he liked to say. I am always grateful for his company.

    This day though, I didn't need any extra motivation. I was excited to be headed to Saratoga. If I'm well enough I spend every August up there with friends and family, and immerse myself in the world of horseracing. The countryside up there is one of my favorite places in the world. Anyone who knows me even slightly will tell you that for a month leading up to the trip I'm like a kid on Christmas morning, jumping around, asking when he can open his presents.

    I'm glad that I'm still able to get that excited about these trips. I look forward to being out amongst those green pastures and the cold lakes of almost transparent blue water, with the smell of horses and hay and timber in my nose. I feel pangs of happiness when I know that I will soon be with many of the people I hold most dear, laughing and breaking bread together. I smile when I know that soon I will breathe cool clean mountain air, and have nothing on my mind except what ponies I might bet on that afternoon, what I might be having for dinner after the races finish, and wondering if my bloodstock agent Lincoln Collins has found us some promising new horses to purchase. I feel truly blessed, knowing that the simplest and purest things in life will all be brought together for a month, unencumbered by the distractions of everyday life and, in my case, everyday disease.

    In Saratoga all the noise surrounding my cancer seems to disappear, at least for a little while. Sure it's always in the back of my mind, but it doesn't insist upon itself and call for my undivided attention, the way it does back home. It's as if in crossing one of those New York highways, we also cross some invisible barrier so that I can enjoy my time up north unencumbered.

Bags in trunk, I hopped in the car eager to go. For me the road trips themselves, both up and back, are an integral part of the experience. This includes stopping in Kentucky midway to see Lincoln and his very able assistant, Freda. We also always take time to visit our friend Buddy Teveens, the Dartmouth football coach, in Hanover, New Hampshire.

We have a routine: Matthew drives up, and later on his younger brother Andrew joins us to take us back to New Orleans. There is some debate as to who is the better driver. Andrew claims the crown, although I don't think that is a decision that even their father, Judge Waldron, would be able to rule on.

Our route takes us up through Tennessee. We stop for the night in Nashville, then drive through Kentucky, West Virginia and Pennsylvania. I had never been to most of these places before I began taking this road trip. Each time I passed through I was struck by the rugged, provincial beauty. When most people think of West Virginia they think of coal miners. After having seen these states firsthand, I think of rolling hills and small towns nestled in the crooks of flowing lakes, and smoky skies that grow even smokier at dusk. The drives have been like an education in the overlooked parts of my country. Hell, we even got to drive up to Niagara Falls, and I enjoyed it without having to get married—but I can see why it's such an appealing destination for weddings and honeymoons. Far better than Las Vegas!

With our fascination with sports, Matthew and I always make a point of visiting the football fields of colleges we pass along the way. We will stop at any school we think looks interesting. They don't have to be powerhouse names. Mid Vermont Christian School is one of the high school athletic fields I particularly enjoyed visiting which no one else would likely stop at. Of course, when we have the chance to go up to Dartmouth, my favorite, we always take it. I like the way Matthew and I meander north. Our plans are always flexible and our friendship allows for spontaneity to shine through.

But we were not quite on the road yet. Matthew had lifted my suitcases into the trunk of my Lexus, while Susan ran through last minute directives. "Make sure you take your medication," she instructed me.

"You'll be up there yourself in a few days," I said. "What's there to worry about?" I was certainly looking forward to Susan joining us shortly in Saratoga.

"I worry," she said. "You know I worry." It felt good that she had my welfare in mind, even when I was not in her immediate care.

"Time to go," I said, sliding into the passenger seat. I was beyond ready to get this show on the road.

"Not quite," Matthew said. "Where's your water?"

"Right here," Susan replied, handing Matthew a large bottle of Dasani. I rolled my eyes. These two were always getting on me about being dehydrated, especially Matthew. "Can't I at least have a Vitamin Water or something that tastes good," I protested.

"That junk is full of sugar," Matthew replied, placing the bottle in my cup holder and starting the engine.

"Okay fine, Coach," I said.

"Y'all drive safe now," Susan called as we pulled out of the driveway.

From the passenger window I watched the beautiful houses of the Garden District slip by, then give way to the streamlined concrete of Interstate 10. Matthew hit the gas, and the Lexus accelerated into the fast lane. We were on the road, heading north to greener pastures.

The first night was spent in Nashville. Early the next morning we continued on into Kentucky, passing through Louisville, then heading east toward Shelbyville. We were now in real horse country. Many of the trainers I worked with over the years had been based out of this area, and the quality of these expert horsemen was almost unmatched. As we drove along I thought about the Hinkle family. They had helped me enormously in my early days in the horse business, and owned a farm nearby. It was a gorgeous place. Nothing fancy, but they raised exceptional horses there. As we got closer to the Hinkle's place, Matthew eyed me with a curious look.

"You want to stop by the farm, Richard?"

"No," I replied. "It wouldn't be the same since Mrs. Hinkle passed away."

"That's true, but it still might be nice."

"Let's just keep driving on to Midway," I said.

"No problem. But in her honor I think we ought to say a little something about Mrs. Hinkle."

"Right, Matty. I can say that she taught me more about horses than anyone I ever met. Except maybe Lincoln."

"Very few people know as much about horses as Lincoln," Matthew replied.

"She was a great woman."

"I think the thing I liked best about her was that she was a person who was sure of her place in the world," Matthew noted. His voice grew serious, hardening into the tone he used on the playing field. "She got the best out of herself, and others wanted to do the best by her. You remember how much of a trooper you were for her, couple of summers ago?"

"Oh, I remember."

"You showed real grit. Not many people would have made it to her funeral after being diagnosed with cancer, but *you* did. I'll always remember that, and I'll always be glad we were there that day."

I nodded and took a sip of water for good measure. Matthew was referring to the summer of 2013, when we had driven to Kentucky for Mrs. Hinkle's memorial service. It was still relatively early in my treatment, and I was struggling with the adverse side effects of both the two sessions of chemotherapy and the ongoing radiation. I hadn't yet met Dr. Tufaro, or been up to Johns Hopkins, and was still relying on local doctors. My health wasn't actively dangerous at that point, but it was far from ideal.

At the time Matthew said that it would be good for me to get out of New Orleans. I had missed the last two summers at Saratoga and he felt I could use a positive jolt to my system. What better way than to honor Mrs. Hinkle? I agreed. If any trip should be my first in two years, it should be that one. So the two of us drove up to her family farm. It was a beautiful service, one that honored the gumption and intelligence of her spirit.

Afterwards, I thought another proper way of paying homage to Mrs. Hinkle would be to watch a race in her living room, where both Matthew and I had spent so many hours listening to her talk about horses. Everyone agreed that would be a perfect idea, especially since I owned a horse that was racing that day. We turned on the television and crowded around, enjoying that tension-filled moment when the horses are lined up and the starting gun is fired.

Wouldn't you know it—my horse came in first place! My eyes grew wide as everyone slapped me on the back and cheered "For Mrs. Hinkle!" That was a much-needed magical moment to lighten our spirits right after the memorial, one of those times where the hand of God seems to intercede into the affairs of man. While there is some doubt as to God's interest in horse races, there was no doubt in my mind that Mrs. Hinkle was looking down on us in that same room where we had been with her for so many good times in years past.

Much to my sorrow, Mrs. Hinkle's son, Sam Hinkle, my great friend in Shelbyville, Kentucky, and a fraternity brother to my cousin John Carrere, passed away just this year from pancreatic cancer. Many times I visited Sam and his wife Kate, and always managed to take some of their children to the Kentucky Derby, something I really looked forward to. He and his family were always wonderful to me. I will miss him dearly as much as I will miss Bronson Thayer. Those are two men I tremendously admired and they will always be in my heart.

"That was a heck of a day," I said to Matthew, still lost in my memory.

"Days like that are what it's all about," he replied.

"Well let's go make some more memories," I said, slapping my hand on the dash.

"Should we go see Lincoln?"

"Damn right we should."

Matthew piloted the Lexus onto the turnoff for Midway, Kentucky, where Lincoln had his office. On the way, I called him on his cell.

"Richard Colton!" he answered in his dignified English accent. Don't ask me how a posh Englishman ended up buying and selling horses in rural Kentucky. That's another book.

"Lincoln, Matty and I are coming to see you. Let's get a couple of steaks."

"It is that time of year, isn't it? Headed up to Saratoga, are we?"

"You betcha."

We met Lincoln at the place in Midway where we always had lunch. It seems all of my friends are culinary creatures of habit, which suits me just fine. Lincoln was in a great mood, tickled pink by a big sale he had just pushed through, and optimistic about the racing at Saratoga that summer. "Going to be a good season," he assured us. "Lots of world-class horses vying for a few moments of glory."

"When will you be up?" I asked.

"In a week or so. Have a few odds and ends to tie up at the office. You going to stay the full month?" Lincoln asked.

"Sure I am," I said. "Been feeling a lot better. Plus I brought Matty here along for insurance."

"Richard's not going to be heading home early, if I've got any say in the matter," Matthew contributed, just as the waiter came to hand us menus and take our drink orders.

"We're back in the game this year," I said.

"Good show," Lincoln replied, exaggerating his accent for effect.

After lunch Matthew and I drove for a few more hours, then found a nice hotel to settle into for the night. The next morning we would head northeast, through the mines and rivers of West Virginia, then cross over to the farms of Amish Pennsylvania and on up into New York State. I was looking forward to every moment of it.

***

Saratoga Springs: August 2016

That summer was the best I ever spent at Saratoga Springs. It seemed as if every moment of the day shone with a quiet glory. A terrific rotation of friends and associates drifted through the town. As usual, my cousin Stella and her husband Bronson Thayer were fixtures at the track. Stella, who owned the Tampa Bay Downs, had been around horses longer than any of us. She could pick a winner, and her face really lit up when she spotted one.

During these first few days my nurse, Susan, arrived, and she and Matthew made sure I drank plenty of water, much to my chagrin. About two weeks into the trip his brother Andrew and their dad, Judge Dennis Waldron, joined us. Andrew, a police officer, had recently been promoted, and his father and brother were proud of him. Dennis kept to his legendary exercise schedule even while on vacation, wearing out several pairs of walking shoes.

As for me, I enjoyed feeling more alive than I had in a long time. I felt re-engaged and re-activated in some fundamental way. It was as if my batteries had been dead for a long time and suddenly had been shocked with a powerful charge. Most days I went to the track, bet some winners, bet some losers, watched the Yankees, and had dinner with my best friends every night. We talked each other's ears off. Johns Hopkins and needles and hospital beds felt very far away.

I didn't have any horses racing that year, which was fine with me. To be competitive at Saratoga your horse really has to be among the cream of the crop. If a trainer has forty five good horses he may only bring fifteen or sixteen up to Saratoga to run.

People think of horseracing as being centered around betting, but there is much more to it than that. There's the breeding, the ownership, the camaraderie with the people involved—many of them blue collar, hard-working people who love horses. Besides, if you are in horse racing for the money you are a fool. If you are going to do nothing but race you are going to lose. It is virtually impossible to make money racing horses. I did it because I loved the game. I did it without any thought of making money. I just tried to sell enough horses through Lincoln to be able to stay in the game.

I've thought a lot about what makes horseracing so thrilling. As I said, for me it has virtually nothing to do with the gambling component. When you gamble you only have two options: relief upon winning or despair upon losing. Relief and despair aren't emotions worth chasing after. Real horseracing gives you something else—it gives you hope. In that almost supernatural sequence of moments, as the horses are plunging down the track, you have real true hope that your horse will win and be declared a champion. Believe me, because I know from experience, the hope you feel while your horse charges down the track is ten times as powerful as any happiness you might feel from a purse you collect or a horse you buy.

I was thinking about horses and hope at the track one afternoon when I ran into Lincoln. I told him my theory, and for the most part he agreed.

"I'll tell you," he said. "I don't ever really think about a big gambling win I've had. You know what I think about all the time? When we had our horse Dernier Croise, who won a big race at Churchill Downs, there were more than a hundred thousand people in the crowd that day. You could hear the *hope* in their voices when they screamed."

"The jockey Gary Stevens won it for us that day," I said. As I recalled, it was Oaks Day, which is the day before the Kentucky Derby.

"Indeed. You know that he won a Triple Crown a few years back?"

"Out of our paygrade now I suppose." Lincoln nodded.

"By the way guys, are you planning to visit Keeneland this year?" he wondered.

Keeneland is a racetrack in Kentucky where I had bought and sold the majority of my horses. When I was really deep in the game I would spend a week there with Lincoln. He would point out the horses that looked good, and were possibly better buys than other horses. It's exciting to be there with all the horses. It is a very quick-paced business. Horses there can sell for as much as a million dollars. Or, in our case, two million dollars. One year we had a winning horse named Miss Lodi that had been bred with another valuable horse and was pregnant, or "in foal" as they say. Whoever bought the horse would get a sort of two-for-one deal. I had often commented to Lincoln that someday I really wanted to be able to sell one of my horses for a million dollars. I got my wish—sort of. To my surprise and delight Miss Lodi sold for two million! But I liked to kid Lincoln on his technical lack of a one million dollar sale.

"I'll only go if you think we could sell a horse for a million dollars," I said, nudging him.

"Marvelous, Richard," Lincoln replied in his dry English manner. "Just a marvelous thing to say."

"Well we *still* haven't sold a horse for a million dollars," I replied.

* * *

One day, towards the end of August, Lincoln, the Waldrons and I decided that we should all go to a Yankees game. We bought the tickets from a company I often use, printed them out at home, and put them in a clear plastic manila folder that I was tasked to hold onto. We left Saratoga in the morning and took the train down to New York City, then caught the subway to the stadium. I was in the last subway car. Along with the folder with the tickets, I was also holding a banana that I bought at the train station in Albany and had not eaten yet.

Lincoln was guiding us as to when we would need to switch trains to get to Yankee Stadium at 161st Street in the Bronx. When he said "now" I rushed off the train, forgetting both the tickets and the banana. Matthew noticed it through the window and chased after the train, but to no avail. It's New York City—I was sure those tickets were gone.

I didn't know what we were going to do, but then a miracle happened. As we are coming up to ground, my cell phone rang. It was a representative of the ticket company, saying that a young gentleman named Anthony Wright had found our tickets and wanted to meet us at the front gates of Yankee Stadium. I couldn't believe what I was hearing—a minor miracle in the Bronx.

We rushed over to the gates and there was a young man waiting for us, waving. He gave us our tickets and said: "Here are your tickets, sir. There's just one problem. I got a little hungry and I ate the banana."

I pulled my wallet out and handed him a hundred dollar bill. Never have I spent one such bill so well. I was happy for Anthony that day and I always wonder what he's doing now. Thanks to him we made it in time for the first pitch. After we finally got settled in the ballpark, I remembered how, six years earlier, we had watched Alex Rodriquez hit his 600th home run in this very same park. I still have the picture we took that day on my dining room wall. That was something! We came close to losing our seats to watch him hit his historic home run. I wrote a letter to Hal Steinbrenner about this incident and unfortunately never got a reply from Hal. I thought it would be nice for the Yankees to recognize Anthony and reward this classy act by a New Yorker. After the game we were in such a good mood that we went for a drink at a nearby Yankees watering hole. The light seemed to glint off the tiles that lined the bar as we settled into our beverages and watched a horse race on the television screens above.

"Hey!" Lincoln suddenly exclaimed. "One of my client's horses is in this race."

We all watched with bated breath as the horses rushed out of the gate and sped down the track.

"Come on!" Lincoln shouted. He stood up in his seat, rocking back and forth. And then, like any horse race, it was over. Lincoln's horse had taken first place. He was so excited that he began to dance a little jig around the bar. Here was this dignified Englishman dancing around a table full of Southerners in a Yankee bar in New York City.

The summers spent up at Saratoga are full of stories like that. That's what happens when you get good people together in a good place. You end up with something greater than the sum of its collective parts. You end up with a life worth living. It's a life you are ready to fight for when you eventually have to return to reality.

***

A little while later, still in the country and still in the dog days of August, my cousin Bronson asked me if I wanted to go to a baseball game with him. There was a minor league team up there that he liked: the Hudson Valley Tri-Valley Cats.

"Sure," I said. "Should I invite the gang?"

"No," he said. "Just me and you, Richard."

I knew that meant Bronson felt like talking about things he couldn't talk about with other people. We had a bond that only people with cancer share. You have an immediate closeness with someone which can't really be replicated in other human interactions. There are of course other relationships you have that can be just as deep and meaningful, but deep in a different way. Cancer carries a sort of shared pain that you can immediately recognize in a kindred soul's eyes.

That day at the ballpark Bronson gave the guy seating everyone a fifty dollar bill, and suddenly we were sitting in great seats. "I should have just told him we're dying of cancer. Then we might have gotten these seats for free," Bronson laughed.

That joke may seem crude, but it's the sort of thing that brings you great relief when you actually *have* cancer. "I think it's pretty obvious that I have *something*," I shot back.

Bronson laughed and we settled into the game, watching, in the late afternoon light, men who wanted to make it in the big leagues try to hit home runs.

"Damn, Richard," Bronson said. "I'm going to miss this."

"Me too," I said. "We'll be back next year."

"Maybe."

"Why? Do you have other plans?"

"It's not so much that *I* have other plans, but that the universe may have other plans for *me*."

"You're doing great," I told him. "We're going to be back

next year, sitting right here, watching these minor league bums try to play baseball."

"Maybe," Bronson repeated.

"Look, all we can do is keep fighting," I said. "Keep going to the best doctors we can find."

"Sometimes the best just isn't good enough."

"Well, that's all we've got. And we've got each other too," I reminded him.

"Damn right we do," he replied, his eyes brightening. "Sorry for being morose. You know how it gets sometimes. You feel like you're climbing Everest without snow shoes."

"Oh, I know it."

"Well, once we get home, please call me anytime you feel like."

"Same goes for you."

It made sense that Bronson wanted to discuss his disease and his mortality. The summer was over. We were heading back to our real lives. Soon there would be doctors and IVs and machines that beeped all night and the Goon Squad and everything else that came with cancer. One of those things was the possibility of death. We both had stage four cancer, so death was something tangible that we felt nipping at our heels.

I don't think either of us realized how closely death was following us. Shortly after I returned home to New Orleans that fall, I was told that my cancer had returned and that I would need a third surgery. I was so thankful that I could pick up the phone and call Bronson, as I did many times that fall, as we commiserated with each other and tried to cheer each other up.

In early December a letter came in the mail from him. I

had undergone the aforementioned surgery, and was still recovering. Receiving a letter from someone close who knew what I was going through was a tremendous comfort. It was like seeing your station appear in the window of a train after a long journey. I had been talking with Bronson by phone and had sent him photos of my Christmas tree. I was a bit extravagant with my decorations that year. I figured now that my cancer had returned I didn't know how many more times I would get to watch those lights twinkle as I listened to the Yankees announcer John Sterling calling games.

Bronson's letter read as follows:

```
December 8
Dear Dick:
   It was great to talk with you tonight and
your voice was so strong. We could tell that
the operation at Hopkins was a great success.
I hope that the report from the pathology
department is equally productive.
   And your Christmas tree looks great. I had
not yet seen it when we talked. It is really
beautiful. We will talk before Christmas +
after my return from Hopkins about December 17
or 18.
   Please send my best to the Waldrons—all of
them. Matt called me 2x as he was in Tampa for
both of his refereeing jobs. I was so sick that
I could not get to either one. Matt is really
doing well—clearly the sky is the limit.
   Best wishes, keep recovering + stay in
touch.
```

> Bronson
>
> Ps: How about BAC! Patience paid off.

I would not get a chance to speak to him when he got out of the hospital in late December. I never got the chance because he passed away that Christmas Eve in 2016. He had been much sicker than he had let on to me, and cancer finally took him on the holiest time of the year. I like to think that his last hours were filled with warm Yuletide images: family close around him, and perhaps even the photos of my Christmas tree.

I have that last letter from Bronson framed and hanging in my house. On the surface it may seem like a simple note containing nothing out of the ordinary, just the news of the day between old friends. To me it is so much more. It is an encapsulation of how Bronson, even in his last days on Earth, was concerned with the normal goings on of life—which is, of course, the stuff that really matters. He didn't wax poetic about mortality or his place in the universe. When you're as close to death as Bronson was you see things clearly. Whenever he discussed his disease he did so in a matter-of-fact way, only mentioning that it had inhibited him from doing something totally normal, like watching Matthew Waldron referee a football game. When you're dying of cancer, just about the best thing in the world would be to go out and watch a simple sports game being called by a friend of yours. I know I've done that, with Matthew refereeing, many times myself.

Bronson's letter demonstrates the importance of not letting cancer define you, and instead using it to define all the other things that are important to you. When your time is limited, what matters is suddenly thrown into stark relief.

For both Bronson and me, what mattered was incredibly simple: spending time with people who are important to us. Really that's what Saratoga Springs was all about. Sure, the horses, the pageantry, the beautiful surroundings and the delicious meals were all well and good. But what's truly important were the people who were there. The Waldrons, Bronson and Stella, Lincoln, Susan—all of us just sharing simple moments together.

If my experiences with cancer have taught me anything, it's this: we have to cling to one another, and hold on even tighter when the circumstances of our lives try to pull us apart.

* * *

Bronson's letter

5

Visible and Invisible Ailments

Pelham, New York, September 2016

Andrew Waldron drove the Lexus up Loren Avenue, a quiet street lined with tall oak trees, and parked across from a large brick house. I recognized the place immediately. In the fall daylight, my boyhood home looked different than how I always remembered it. It had aged in some strange way, yet there was no mistaking it as the place where I had spent my formative years.

"Richard, I think this is it," Andrew said, pointing out the car window.

"Yes," I replied, my mind already flooded with memories. "We've found it."

In keeping with our tradition, after his brother Matthew had driven me up to Saratoga Springs at the beginning of the summer, Andrew was now driving me back down to New Orleans. Instead of making a straight shot down to Louisiana, however, we decided to pay a visit to Pelham, New York, the town where I grew up. I still had my old address and, as the summer was ending, I for some reason felt like re-exploring the town of my youth on this particular return trip.

Pelham is a sleepy little hamlet of twelve thousand residents just twenty miles north of New York City. Most people who live there commute into the big city for work, as my father did for many years. Here, residents enjoy a tranquil sort of existence that recalls a bygone era of baseball games, good schools, and neighbors who actually know your name. The area is a slice of suburban American pie still relatively untouched by the complications and machinations of the "city that never sleeps," only a relatively few miles away.

Andrew and I were parked just across the street from the house where I had spent ages seven to eighteen. How long had it been since I had last seen this house? Forty years? Fifty? That immense span of time seemed to condense as I sat in the car with Andrew, transported back in time to 1950, when I was only seven years old. Suddenly I could picture myself back at our kitchen table in the morning, seated across from my mother as she fussed over *The New York Times* crossword puzzle. I could smell bacon being fried by our housekeeper, Mary Campbell. I could hear my father's key turning in the lock at night as he walked in the door, home from a long day's work in the city.

Memories rushed over me like images from a motion picture—snapshots immersing me in a past that the tricky sands of time had buried. For many of us, certain sights, smells or sounds can bring those memories back. Seeing my childhood home certainly had that effect on me. As I looked around, a strange feeling took hold of me: the emotions attached to those memories were laden with meaning, some joyful, others with more than a dose of melancholy.

My family had first moved to Pelham in 1945. This house on Loren Avenue was actually the second home there. I don't have many memories of that earlier time, as I was only about two years old, but I do know that we initially lived on a street called Windward Road. After only a couple of years there my father moved our family out of Pelham to a town near Philadelphia. He had gotten a job with RCA Victor, which was in the process of bringing color televisions to the average American home. It may seem antiquated now, when everyone has a mobile computer in his or her pocket, but in the late 1940s color televisions were a big deal—a symbol of progress as well as prosperity. My father supervised the freight distributions all over the country and was extremely successful in his position.

I believe that job was important to him, as it proved to himself and others that he could make it on his own, be his own man. You see, my mother's side of the family were the founders of Lykes Brothers Inc., a major shipping and land-owning corporation that had been in operation since 1910. My father obviously felt the need to demonstrate that he could succeed in providing for his wife and child independent of the Lykes establishment.

I think that was an honorable thing my father did, both for himself and his family, to achieve something on his own. To his credit he succeeded, which would always be a point of pride for him. Looking back, it was one of the best lessons he taught me: how to be your own man, despite outside pressure, and the very real possibility of failure.

Eventually, the Lykes company did manage to persuade my dad to come work for them in New York. So in 1950 he moved our family back to Pelham—this time to the house on Loren Avenue I visited that day in 2016 with Andrew Waldron. My family had settled in rather quickly. My father was even elected mayor of the district we lived in, Pelham Heights. One of his first ordinances was to mandate that people had to use leashes when walking their dogs. My mother sure had to field a lot of unhappy phone calls to the house about that!

But it was indicative of who my father was as a person. When he believed something should be done a certain way he stuck to it steadfastly. No matter what.

My mother was a different sort of soul: gentler, kinder, more intellectual. Since my father worked long hours in the city, most of my childhood hours were spent with her. I had and will always have a tremendous amount of affection for my mother. She was a literary-minded person, always immersed in books and newspapers. She was the crossword puzzle champion of our town. I remember that everyone in the neighborhood would call her by Wednesday to see if she had finished the *Sunday Times* crossword puzzle, which was and still is no small feat. My job was to help her answer the sports questions, since it was a subject of little interest to her and I usually knew the answers.

Sports were everything to me. I remember playing stickball every day with kids my age who lived down the street. Soon I progressed to the other things boys my age were interested in, such as pro wrestling. I loved to go to Madison Square Garden to watch the professional wrestlers. I was also obsessed with the Yankees, then and now, as I'm sure you already know. My grandpa, who lived right down the street from us, would take me to games. I also listened to Yankee games on my radio when I should have been sleeping.

As I said, my father worked long hours and I didn't get to see as much of him as I did my grandfather. Perhaps it was better that way. My mother and grandpa treated me like an adult. They never talked down to me. That's a great lesson my mother taught me, to always talk to other people like he or she is your equal. Same with my grandfather. He'd always talk to me man to man. I try to be like that myself.

My dad was the opposite. His way of treating me was more like bullying. That didn't work well for our relationship. But I don't entirely blame him. It was unfortunately all too common with men of that era. Many friends who grew up in that same time have reported a similar experience. Fathers felt like they had to be a certain way—hard-nosed and competitive—and it adversely affected their relationships with their sons.

I'll give you an example. My dad loved to host cookouts. On weekends, that was one of his favorite things to do. He was terrific on the grill. He would pass a big steak around to everyone. I appreciated that he loved to grill, and I always looked forward to it because that meant he would be home, and that I would get to spend some time with him.

One afternoon he had a bunch of his friends over for a barbecue. I wanted to show him that I was an adult, one of the guys, so I picked up some of the Lykes company's shipping materials and began to read it on a picnic table near where he was grilling. I was really focused on the materials when all of a sudden I heard his booming voice saying: "Richie is over there reading this stuff on the company, but I know he can't understand any of it."

I felt like a rain cloud had come to a halt right over my head. There I was, trying to show him that I cared about the family company by taking a real interest in it, and he could do nothing but insult me. Those sort of incidents didn't happen every day, but they also weren't uncommon. That took a toll on our relationship, and on the way I viewed my father.

As I said, I tended to relate more to my mother. Even though she didn't have any real interest in wrestling, basketball and other things with which I was obsessed, she still respected my interests. Once she went with me when I entered a basketball free-throw competition near my local elementary school. I made seven out of ten baskets, which I thought was pretty good. What made me happy is knowing that my mother would not have cared if I made ten or zero; she stood by me while I attempted to do something that was important to me. I'll always love her for moments like that.

I'm not trying to say that I harbor some deep resentment toward my father, nor that I blame him for anything in my life. In fact, quite the opposite. I actually grew closer to him as we got older, and came to better understand the position he had to inhabit in the world. It's not easy being a high-powered businessman. I learned that as soon as I entered that world myself. My father and I grew closest once I also began working for the Lykes company. We were able to inhabit each other's worlds, and have a better comprehension of each other as individuals and as men. By the time my father reached old age, and until he passed on, our relationship had reached a good place. I think that is very common of fathers and sons, especially fathers and sons of that time. We simply didn't have the language to communicate with each other when I was a boy. I'm glad we found it when I got older.

"Richard, you there?" I heard Andrew's voice coming to me through a fog, jarring me back to the present from the realm of memory.

"Yes," I said. "Sorry I was just…"

"I know," he said. "Must take you back."

"Sure does," I replied. Then he drove us away.

The rest of that day Andrew and I visited various other places from my childhood. We saw my grade school and my church, and had a meal at the country club to which my family had once belonged. It was a deeply affecting afternoon. I was glad to have Andrew's steady policeman presence and demeanor by my side. Memory has a funny way of sneaking up on you, uncovering things which you thought you had long since moved on from.

***

New Orleans, September 2016

By the time Andrew and I arrived back to New Orleans, I was in a bit of a funk. Traveling so far into my past, recalling all those memories of my childhood, especially of my complicated relationship with my father, had thrown my emotions into a swirl of confusion. Other recollections, those concerning my time working for the family business, had begun to nibble at the corners of my mind, like pesky mice. Those thoughts triggered even more complex and uncomfortable feelings.

Andrew, who is quieter than his brother Matthew, but no less attuned to people's moods, noticed that I had turned inward during the last part of the drive. "Make sure you keep your head up, Richard," he told me simply, but with an underlying supportive warmth, as we pulled up in front of my home.

"I'll try," I replied, opening the Lexus' door and stepping out. I already felt far away from Andrew, as if a fog had settled between us. It had nothing to do with him: I had simply begun a retreat into my own past, my mind busy sorting out all kinds of memories that lay dormant for so long.

We carried my bags into the house and said our goodbyes. As soon as Andrew left, the melancholy I felt in the car redoubled and mounted into full-on depression. I slumped in a chair and clicked the television on, hoping for a Yankee game. No such luck. I sighed again, negative feelings tugging at my brain.

This is difficult to admit, but since my early thirties I have struggled with clinical depression. Although by 2016 I already had achieved a comfortable handle on the condition over many years, in all honesty each time I returned to New Orleans from Saratoga I would often slip back into spells of dejection which, thankfully, were always temporary. It wasn't Saratoga. Saratoga was a place filled with so much life, so many friends, so many good times, that the harsher realities of my current existence, especially these days, my precarious state of health, always seemed to dissipate when I was there. However, when I came back home, these depressive feelings frequently returned with a force that was difficult to defend against.

This latest trip had been especially indicative of the negative impact on my psyche in coming back from Saratoga. On the one hand, this past year up there had been one of the most beautiful and impactful times I ever shared with my racing associates and buddies. On the other hand, now that I was back in New Orleans I was even more conscious of my dire cancer diagnosis, and the fact that summer was over and I might not live to see another one. In addition to that, confronting my childhood in Pelham, even though most of my memories were positive, had been an intense experience.

Sitting alone in my house, my mind raced. I found myself thinking back to the time I had spent with the Lykes company. How did I really feel about those years? And how did my complex and contradictory memories of my father connect to the many years of my life I had spent working with him in the shipping business? Suddenly I was again lost in the mist of bygone years.

There had never really been any doubt in my mind, perhaps not in my family's as well, that I would one day work for the Lykes corporation. When you come from a large family that founded a huge, successful company, it is inevitable that you feel a certain loyalty, and a strong sense of duty, toward upholding what your predecessors built. Shortly after college I did go to work for Lykes, in the marketing department of the steamship company. I was very successful, always felt respected by my peers, and eventually was put on special assignment for the company in Japan. I lived in Japan for over two years, doing sales work and brokering deals between our company and various overseas Asian agencies.

In case you are wondering right about now, it is not my intention to catalogue my entire career at Lykes. My reason for bringing up my role in the family business is to relate how the time spent there fueled my depression—eventually leading to a dramatic episode at the age of thirty-nine. I view my time at Lykes, and this episode, as central to my purpose in life and my growth as an individual. For the purpose of this life story I share with you now, I believe my struggles against depression provide a background that will help you understand how I overcame many of my fears with regard to my ongoing fight against the deadly form of cancer that kept my continued survival in question.

While I was in Japan I began to feel that I was being left out of the decision-making process at the company. I decided that being thousands of miles away was a handicap; that if I came back I would have a greater say in the business's day-to-day functions. This reasoning turned out to be false and returning was a mistake. In hindsight I should have remained in Japan, where I was learning a tremendous amount about overseas shipping practices and international business. What I discovered when I returned to New Orleans was that there was no prominent role for me in the main office. I was still useful, of course, but felt I had somehow taken a wrong turn.

I can pinpoint how, around this time, my full-out depression began to manifest. A silent spectre at first, its tendrils began to creep their way into many aspects of my life. I was not as motivated as I had once been. I let things slip through the cracks. I simply didn't feel the same *fire* I had felt as a younger man. I was now acting purely out of a sense of obligation to my family, the family company, and my name.

Compounding this negativity was the discovery that I was no longer being seriously considered to become chairman of the company. This was a role I had always thought of as possible for myself, though in truth not one I lusted after. It was an option I thought I *should* go after because of my position in the family, and because of the fierce loyalty I know I had shown for years. However, after returning from Japan and being placed in a lesser position than I had expected, this now seemed like an unrealistic possibility.

While working at Lykes, an ambitious colleague, seeing that I was part of the Lykes family and had an executive position, came to me with a request that we work closely together on some interesting business deals. He felt sure, he said, that I was the right one to one day take over the chairmanship of the company; thus he was confident that the success of these projects could elevate both of our positions in the company.

At that point I couldn't even assure *myself*, let alone a colleague, that I would someday become chairman. I certainly could have played this a bit better and worked with this gentleman. Perhaps not doing those deals was not in my best interests back then. But, looking back with hindsight, I still believe I made the right decision. Maybe not in terms of rising in the company, but certainly in terms of becoming the person I eventually intended to become.

Others could view this as a lack of confidence, and apparently they did. I think now that in turning down that deal-making I was subconsciously guiding myself away from the role of business leadership and turning more towards the artistic journey by which the rest of my life has been guided.

Nonetheless, after that incident I began to feel increasingly isolated at Lykes. I wasn't getting the kind of support from my fellow coworkers that I believed I should have. That doesn't mean I didn't feel respected by them, because that was something I always felt. I just felt *alone*, as though I was on an island by myself. Although I didn't realize it, my depression was becoming more severe.

Depression is a sneaky enemy. Often it has you ensnared before you are aware of the danger you're in.

All of these factors came to a head in the dramatic incident I alluded to earlier. It happened shortly after my thirty-ninth birthday. We had scheduled a regular weekly meeting with some of our competitors. These weekly meetings were routine stuff to discuss and justify freight rates which were allowed under the Federal Maritime Commission. Throughout my career I had held hundreds of meetings like this. That morning began like any other. I checked into the office for my messages, saw that everything was running smoothly, then made my way to the conference room where the meeting was to take place.

As was my habit, I was early. I watched as the other executives filtered in, greeting one another and shaking hands.

Soon enough everyone was seated around the table, and I took a seat next to my compatriots from Lykes. It was a fairly standard meeting, but when it was my turn to speak and I made my suggestions, none of my coworkers spoke up in support of what I proposed. As I continued to talk, it began to feel like everyone was on one side and I was on the other. Nonetheless, I continued to make my pitch in support of my ideas, standing up and facing the room. Suddenly, I became completely unaware of what I was saying. All I could focus on was the room full of faces staring at me; endless pairs of eyes that seemed to be boring into me, dissecting me, making me feel completely and totally alone.

In that moment I lost consciousness. I remember the swaying lights above me that grew brighter. I recall seeing the ceiling swim toward me as I fell to the ground. However, I don't remember much more after that, just a sea of faces and loud voices shouting: "Richard, Richard!" Then everything went black.

When I woke up I found myself lying in a hospital bed. For the next month I would remain in the hospital, recovering from whatever it was that caused me to lose my equilibrium. After a battery of tests, it became clear that what literally brought me down was mental, not physical. At that time the primary emotion I felt was embarrassment. I didn't have the language to understand or talk about the depression I was feeling—I just felt I had failed. Many people from the company came to visit me. I would just lie in bed, pretending to be asleep so I couldn't see or hear them. Eventually they stopped visiting, which is what I wanted. During this time I sank even deeper into angst over what I perceived as my many failures.

The one person who was able to get through to me was a colleague named Barton Jahncke. When Barton visited me in the hospital his demeanor wasn't like the other visitors, or even like the doctors who tended me. He was calm. He treated me like an equal and an intelligent person, much as my mother and grandpa had when I was a boy.

Sitting by the edge of my bed, he put his hat on his knee. "You don't have to come back if you don't want to, Richard," he said. "You don't have anything to prove to anyone."

That moment of understanding and permission from someone I liked and respected was a breakthrough for me. I realized that, first and foremost, I had to get better for *myself*, and for the next six months that's exactly what I did. I saw a psychiatrist. I saw another therapist. I learned a whole new language that helped me understand and be able to discuss what I had been going through for years but had never before been able to articulate. I exercised more. I talked to my mother. I talked to my father. But most importantly, I *listened* to myself.

It's easier for me to talk about such things now than as a younger man. In that "Mad-Men" era, talking about depression, for me at least, but I think also for many others, would have been unthinkable. People viewed depression as a weakness. Today I refuse to view it that way. The traumas you go through can help you grow. They have made me a stronger and better man. Certainly I would rather be the man I am today than some automaton in a suit, going through the motions at a job in which I had no real investment. It takes courage to admit you need help, and takes strength to admit you need to make significant changes in your life, in spite of what other people think is right for you.

After about six months of treatment, and taking good care of myself, I returned to Lykes. I was glad then and am glad now that *I did* go back. I no longer felt I had anything to prove, but I also felt I did a good thing by returning. Some people said I was *too* loyal—loyal to a fault. To me it felt like unfinished business, that I still owed some duty toward myself and towards what my family had built. Once I went back I established myself in ways I never had previously, spearheading an entirely new division in marketing. I never made chairman, but I stayed with the company for another twenty years.

I left my position at the Lykes company in 1995. The company was moving to Tampa, Florida, and wanted me to move along with it. I told them I wasn't leaving New Orleans. I had been there for decades and had no intention of uprooting my life. So that was that. I was fifty-six years old, with many years in front of me. I remember feeling elated, with a new sense of freedom. A huge part of my life had ended and a larger part was about to start.

It may sound strange, but I truly believe that my life *really* began when I left the company. Up to that point I had been living mainly under an umbrella of loyalty and responsibility. While those are not negative cornerstones on which to build a life, I know now that they also closed the door to a lot of individuality and personal development. My relationship to the Lykes company had been a complex one, tied up with the history of my family and the duty I felt toward them. There is a price for everything, including loyalty. I paid the price, but I also got to reap benefits.

In writing this book, I will tell you candidly that I did struggle with whether I could or should expose this highly personal part of myself. I decided to do so because I think it is important to show what I went through, and overcame. This particular struggle will hopefully show you how I became the kind of person who could endure what cancer took from me, and how I am able to live as fully and fearlessly as I do. Yes, I temporarily succumbed to an extreme bout of depression that almost took me down completely. But cancer tried to do the same, and both failed. Depression and cancer are very different ailments, but you have to fight against both every single day in order to survive, not only physically but also spiritually. You have to be a *fighter*. I like to think I am.

What I didn't know, after I left Lykes with such enthusiasm and excitement for the life ahead, was that even as so many wonderful things began to happen for me in many areas, in other ways the real fight of my life had only just begun.

* * *

88 *No More. No Less.*

6

Do You Know What It Means To Love New Orleans?
New Orleans, November 2016

I have called New Orleans home for more than five decades and hope to do so for years to come—God willing, as they say. But to some "natives" even that length of time doesn't qualify me as a "true" New Orleanian. To deserve that designation I would have had to have been born here, and never lived anywhere else for longer than a vacation. Yet those who know me know that my heart, soul, and roots are as deeply entrenched here as are the native. I have tried to contribute to this city to the best of my ability. In turn it has fed my mind and spirit, and blessed me with more friendships than I can count.

If you truly love a place, as I do New Orleans, you feel a certain poignant absence every moment you are separated from its soil. That same sentiment is what Louis Armstrong, the Big Easy's most cherished and celebrated son, articulated when he crooned these words: *Do you know what it means to miss New Orleans/ When that's where you left your heart/ And there's one thing more, I miss-the one I care for/ More than I miss New Orleans/ The moonlight on the bayou, a Creole tune that fills the air/ I dream about magnolias in bloom and I'm wishin' I was there.*

Armstrong's voice and lyrics powerfully express the intense devotion every New Orleanian feels towards the city's uncommon images, storied history, unparalleled eccentricities, and unique attitude. It is a passionate city, one where people cheer as loudly for their Saints in the Superdome as they do for a jazz band playing a late night song on Frenchman Street. It is a city filled with sultry nights in the French Quarter, where you feel like you've stepped back into a time that was both more elegant and more charmingly delinquent.

As you ride Uptown through the streets on the iconic St. Charles streetcar, past the manicured mansions and storied cemeteries of the Garden District, your soul cannot help but be stirred by the knowledge that this same line of streetcars have carried such famous residents as Fats Domino, Truman Capote, Allen Toussaint, Leah Chase, Elmore Leonard and other legendary people to their destinations. All of these remarkable individuals have added their own flavor to the New Orleanian gumbo: a stew as delicious and irresistible as those cooked up in any kitchen, whether home or local restaurant.

New Orleans is a city of extremes. Weather-wise, it can get so hot and humid here in mid-August that the mosquitoes call it quits and move up north. Other times a cold snap moves in. At times there are so many inebriated tourists careening up and down Bourbon Street that the policemen find their holding cells seriously overcrowded. For every beautiful old home in the Garden District there is a blighted property in the Ninth Ward that has not been restored since the levees burst during Hurricane Katrina.

Like other major cities, here too there is massive wealth and massive poverty. There are meals at *Brennan's* that cost one hundred dollars a head, and tiny hole in the wall poor-boy joints with sandwiches that cost three bucks, both equally delicious. There is dysfunction in our local government, and at the same time we have the purest form of community where our residents often come together to help each other. On Sundays both barrooms and churches are full to the brim.

Like every other true New Orleanian, I love every corner of my city, contradictions and all. Even these words I set to paper do not do justice to the heart and soul of New Orleans. Perhaps the writer Chris Rose best described the city's enigmatic nature when he wrote: *"It is impossible to capture the essence, tolerance, and spirit of south Louisiana in words, and to try is to roll down a road of clichés, bouncing over beignets and beads and brass bands and it just is what it is. It is home."*

When I think of all the places in my adopted city that are important to me, I have to start with my own home, and work outward. The best starting place that comes to mind is my front porch. I tend to begin and end my days on that porch, sitting in my favorite chair, looking out at the street, pondering my life, and talking with any and everyone who moseys by. From this vantage point I've had some of my most enlightening and surprising encounters, and take pride in knowing that I've become a staple of the neighborhood.

Throughout the years I've met a wide spectrum of people: British tourists making the rounds of Uptown cemeteries, artists trying to make their way in the world, couples walking their honeymoon nights in the twilight. In true New Orleans fashion, however, the most interesting encounters tend to come from people who live in my fair city.

In fact, not too long ago a neighbor of mine provided me with an experience I could have scarcely imagined possible. For privacy's sake her name will be omitted, but my neighbor is a beautiful girl with long flowing hair who often entertains musicians. One evening, sitting on my porch, I caught a glimpse of her just outside my gate. She was always a welcome sight, so I stood up from my seat and waved towards her.

"Richard," she called. "Have I got a surprise for you!"

"Oh yeah?" I asked, going down the front stairs to open the gate for her. "It takes a lot to surprise me at my age. I've seen quite a lot," I challenged jokingly.

"Well you haven't seen this," she replied, motioning forward a young man who stood a few steps away that I hadn't previously noticed. Now I saw that he was smartly dressed, with a sort of sly smile across his face. A musician, as I could already tell.

My neighbor and her associate bounded up my steps. "I want you to meet my friend," she said. "He's Elton John's piano player. Elton is playing in New Orleans this week."

"Is that so?" I replied, shaking his hand. "Well you know I've got quite a piano here."

"I'd be honored to play a tune for you," the young man said, and we all went into my house together. As we entered my foyer, the musician looked up at the large painting of Fats Domino I have hanging right by the front door that I referenced before. It's a vibrant, soulful piece by local painter Terrance Osborne, an artist of great renown and talent whose gallery, located on Magazine Street, filled mainly with local scenes he paints, is one of the finest in the city. His work is in great demand, and I love this painting.

"Don't feel like you have to measure up to Fats," I assured the young man as we passed the massive artwork and proceeded to the piano. "I would never dream of it," he said with a laugh, settling down to the ivories.

As this talented pianist played us a beautiful bevy of

songs, including of course several Elton John numbers, even my old feet begin to tap. The music made my heart swell, and I sat there thinking that only in New Orleans was this sort of spontaneous thing possible. One moment you're sitting on your porch minding your business, and the next moment you may have Elton John's piano player tickling the ivories in your own home.

I've become sort of a fixture here, holding court on the front porch of my grand old home, but I wasn't always in such a luxurious position. Like so many others, I came to New Orleans as a young man, seeking to make something of myself. When I arrived in this city I was only twenty-two years old, fresh out of university and eager to start my career at the Lykes family's company. At the time I didn't know much about New Orleans' rich history. It was simply a blank canvas upon which I could paint my future. What future would that be? I certainly didn't know, but I sure was eager to find out.

John Carrere was extremely helpful. His father, Uncle Jack, got me an apartment, and they both helped me during my early days. That was a small place, far from the Uptown house I live in now. Back then Uncle Jack wanted to see me assimilate into his social world, so he set me up on a date with a girl he knew named Rosemonde Kuntz. I had not had a whole lot of dating experience at that point in my life. I certainly was not yet used to the Southern style. Anyway, Jack lent me his Cadillac to use on the date. It was a real beauty, and frankly I was afraid to drive it in case I might scratch his leather seats. Nonetheless, I drove it to this girl's house and knocked on her door. Rosemond was still upstairs, running late—turned out she was always late. I actually had to wait about twenty or thirty minutes for her to make an appearance.

Finally she came down the stairs, and, to my shocked surprise, she was wearing her mother's mink coat. To be honest, I really felt out of my element. I had no car, and now I was dating a girl who came downstairs in a mink coat.

I must say she was a nice girl. I liked her, and I did try to call her, but every time I tried to call she was either taking a bath or doing something else. Clearly this was just not going to happen. Although we were not meant to be as a romantic couple, Rosemonde actually helped me enter the social scene and make friends in New Orleans. Forty years later we are still best of friends. That says something about the kind of people that live in New Orleans.

New Orleans was then, as it still is now, an entrenched place, in its ways and how it operates. For me it was an adjustment. I was a guy who had moved around a lot. Rosemonde, for one example, had grown up in one house and lived in it all her life. After she got married, wouldn't you know—she and her husband took over the house she grew up in, so she never left it. This is sort of a tradition in New Orleans. Take for example Sherrie Soule, one of the best waitresses from Joey K's, who works with me now, as my awesome executive assistant. She is part of the same Southern story. Sherrie grew up in her childhood home and then raised her kids in the same house. Many women in this city live in the same house in which they grew up. People love where they are from and don't see any reason to change. That is part of the culture for sure. Other young couples get married and then their parents buy them a house *nearby* their childhood home. That's just a way of life down here, and it's not at all bad.

After that first small apartment I moved to a slightly larger place—a small cottage down near the docks where I was working for Lykes. After a couple of years in which I focused on my career, I went into the Coast Guard, and remained there from age twenty three to twenty five. After boot camp, my group was assigned to a ship, and we did weather patrol. What would happen is that we would go out halfway to Hawaii, make circles, and assess the weather movement. For some of us guys that got pretty boring, so several of the guys decided they were going to throw some of our gear overboard. Boy did we get in trouble for that, and rightfully so—what were we thinking!

Soon my service ended, and I was able to go back to the Lykes company. I was moved up from working on the docks to the office. As I related earlier, the company sent me over to Japan on assignment, and, again, I stayed there for nearly two years.

Once I got back into town from abroad, thanks to John and Jack Carrere, Rosemond and others, things started to pick up for me socially. I began to be invited to all the debutante parties. That was great, since I got to meet many prominent families and interesting girls. Many of their parties needed young men to serve as escorts. I was a good dancer, and slowly got past my shyness, which then allowed me to have a great deal of fun at parties. Girls would send out a small card with an invitation that would say: "Please escort Miss Mary Brown." Or just "Please escort Mary Brown." I would call them up and make arrangements. This was not a date per se: it was a little more formal than a date. The same girl could invite you back again, so this scene was driven more by the girls then by the men. I think the girls, to be socially correct and popular, dressed up for each other. As for me, sometimes I would go in a tuxedo; you would definitely be a hit if you wore a tux and could dance. As I said, I was a good dancer at that point in my life. Not doing much dancing these days, but the memories linger.

Swept up in the social scene in those days, I also attended a number of masquerade balls. It was all part of being a young man in New Orleans. This was my real introduction to the city. I would dance with my partner, and have dinner and a few drinks, and socialize. At the end of the night I would drive whatever young lady I was escorting home.

Nancy Nolan was among my frequent dance partners. One of the four Nolan sisters, she liked me, as did the two other Nolan sisters, Nell and Margie, whom I also escorted. The only sister I didn't date was Betty: she had a steady boyfriend who is now her husband. I don't recall why it didn't work out with Nancy, but she was a lot of fun. We always had a good time. Actually I had known Margie when I was in Japan. Margie had gone over to teach for the Sacred Heart School in Taiwan. She was probably the girl I liked best. When I got back home from Japan I realized I should have spent more time with Margie Nolan. I finally called her, but by that time she was traveling with her boyfriend, Julian Wheatley, who later became her husband. She and Julian have lived in New Orleans for the past 13 years. Nell, Margie, Nancy and I have all remained close. Those are the kind of relationships you can have in New Orleans: they last and last in the best way.

In New Orleans there is a high barrier to entry, so to speak. It isn't easy to become friends with someone, but once you are friends it is a lasting friendship. A lot of people have now been my close friends for over thirty years. In other cities, everyone wants to be your friend *immediately*, but few of these "friendships" actually last.

My friendships are the main thing I truly treasure about my city. One of my closest friends in town is Judge Dennis Waldron, whom I have mentioned often; and as I said, we met at Joey K's. Sherrie, who knew the judge well, introduced us one day since she waited on both of us all the time. I was having my usual order of catfish, mashed potatoes, and red beans and rice. Sherrie took the initiative to go up to each of us and tell us separately that she had someone we'd really enjoy meeting. From that day on Dennis and I became great lunch partners, and our friendship blossomed, the way friendships do in New Orleans.

These days Dennis and I still have lunch together almost every day, along with a wonderful, ever-changing crew. We even have a colorful little "reserved" sign on the corner table that Sherrie had made for us by popular local artist Simon. It says "Richard" on one side and "Judge" on the other side. For me Joey K's is "The place where everyone knows your name" as in the TV series *Cheers*. It's the little things like that which make Joey K's such a special place in my life.

Over lunch, my friends and I talk about anything and everything. Sometimes I sit there chewing on my catfish and think: *How lucky can one man be?* I must say that Judge Dennis Waldron has a quiet dignity to him: a quality that makes him an excellent dining partner. He is also an integral part of this city—a central local character. I admire how he keeps to his routine of strict exercise every day so that he can work off those Joey K's calories. Our table, with all of us seated around it, represents various connections to all aspects of the city. Dennis Waldron represents the judicial system. I like to think I represent the art scene and the school system.

Did you scratch your head just now when I said I represent the school system of New Orleans? After all, I am not a teacher. I say that because of something I don't really like to talk about: my philanthropic efforts. When one has been as financially blessed as I have, I feel there's a duty to give back, especially to a city that has given me so much. Over the years—and most especially after I hit one of my lowest points, and made my "contract with God" to, in essence, do more good in the world—or at least my little corner of the world—if God would give me more time, I have expanded a scholarship fund that I set up to help young people attend college and even private high schools. Many of these young people have had serious challenges in their lives, and with these scholarships and the educational support of teachers, counselors and mentors they have been able to turn their lives around. The recipients often do not know where these funds came from. My joy is in helping others anonymously whenever possible. This includes helping young people who had gotten in trouble with the law to hire a good attorney to navigate the system for them. I can tell you with great joy that every one I've helped this way has become an excellent, law-abiding citizen, holding productive full-time jobs or in an exciting career. One of my greatest undertakings, which in this case was *not* done anonymously, because I was so happy and proud to be a visible part of this endeavor, has been to fund a new Arts Center at the Academy of The Sacred Heart.

The Academy of The Sacred Heart is a highly respected all-girls Catholic school. A pillar of the community, this school produces some of the finest young women New Orleans has to offer. A few years back I was attending a sports banquet there for the school's athletics program. I was talking to some of the girls, and they wondered out loud why the sports teams got a banquet each year, but there was no banquet for the arts.

That got me thinking that there was definitely a need to recognize girls, many of whom have real artistic gifts. So I decided to do something about it. I donated money to have an Arts Center built. I am proud to say that it has been formally named the "Richard C. Colton Jr. Center for Performing and Fine Arts." As someone who participates in the art world by supporting up-and-coming artists and collecting fine art, it was important to me to give those girls a chance to be recognized in the areas in which they excel. This umbrella—the arts—encompasses theater, both on stage and behind the scenes skills and talents, including painting, writing, and so much more.

The ability for the arts to flourish at a time when, sad to say, they are no longer in the forefront culturally, or with financial support too often withheld, is a big challenge. It is something we need to keep working on.

Interestingly, Sacred Heart is a generational school. When a mother goes there, usually her daughter does too, and then *her* daughter. I feel proud that the impact of my Arts Center has the potential to span multiple generations and have a serious impact on the arts culture in my city. I never had a daughter of my own, so funding this facility was a way to intertwine my legacy with the children of this city.

All this moved me deeply one day when I went to see the musical, "Shrek," that the girls had put on in this new performing arts center. Walking in, it was strange to see my name over the entranceway, but of course so rewarding. At that time an eighth grade girl named Katherine Wise had the lead in the musical. I sat in the front row, entranced, as she sang the lead number, "When Words Fail." Even now words fail *me* when I think back on the poignancy of that moment. It was overwhelming, as the music and lyrics washed over me, to see all these incredible young women begin to fulfill their life purposes through art and song. I won't admit to weeping, but I won't pretend my eyes were dry. Every time I pass by Sacred Heart on my way to Joey K's or another one of my local haunts, that memory floods my mind. Really, what more can a man ask for in life?

I can't tell you how many people have come up to me over the years to tell me how happy they are to have this performing arts center. That makes me feel even more connected to my community and my city. Many generous people might have thought to put something like this in their Last Will and Testament, but then they would never have been able to experience everything as I have. It is truly a gift to yourself to see this impact while you are alive.

Founding that arts space at Sacred Heart filled a place in my life that had been empty. I didn't have my own daughter to sing me a song, but I sure did get my song sung, and then some, by other sweet and talented daughters. That really is what I want my legacy in this city to be: giving back to the next generation.

My time on earth is limited, but New Orleans will always go on. Artists like Terrance Osborne on Magazine Street will continue to make New Orleans-style art that is unlike any other. The chefs at restaurants like Joey K's, Commander's Palace, and Houston's, another favorite haunt, will continue to make food that frankly can only be best cooked in this city. The horses down at the race track will continue to run, and there will always be winners and losers at the racetrack. The colorful cast of characters that revolves through this city will continue to get up to good, to no good, and to everything in between. The jazz will continue to swing, the mosquitoes will continue to bite, and the Mississippi River will continue to flow. The girls at Sacred Heart will continue to sing.

Now I hope you know what I mean when I say that I love New Orleans.

* * *

Photo Gallery
Early Years

Me at 9 months old, with my mother, Howell Lykes Colton, enjoying a day in the sun, Lake Forest, Illinois. I was born in the Chicago Lying-In Hospital in Chicago.

Me with my favorite radio flyer wagon, 1948.

Me, baby sister Elizabeth, and sister Keenan.

The Gunnery JV basketball team. I was a senior this year, #50. Robert Zavorskas, #24 class of '63, became an outstanding guard on the varsity team. He is a freshman in this photo. The JV team had an excellent record.

Me in my Coast Guard Uniform, late 1960's.

The Gunnery on a summer trip to visit my alma mater. I was in the graduate class of 1960.

With grandpa, Joseph T. Lykes, in Clearwater, Florida after I caught my first fish, which was a flounder. Grandpa was very pleased, while I looked quite serious. I will never forget this picture or this day, 1948.

My Dad, Richard C. Colton Sr. Joins Lykes Bros. Steamship Company

December 13, 1950

Mr. Charles E. Widmayer
Dartmouth Alumni Magazine
Dartmouth College
Hanover, New Hampshire

Dear Mr. Widmayer:

The following, concerning Mr. Richard C. Colton, Dartmouth College Class of '25, will be an interesting item for the next issue of the Alumni magazine:

Richard C. Colton resigned his position as General Traffic Manager of Radio Corporation of America, RCA Victor Division, effective December 31, 1950, to accept a new position as Vice President in Charge of the New York office of Lykes Bros. Steamship Co., Inc. Lykes has been serving exporters and importers via Gulf Ports for fifty years and now own and operate fifty-one fast C-type vessels to and from Gulf Ports and six major world trade routes -- United Kingdom Line, Continent Line, Mediterranean Line, Africa Line, Orient Line and Caribbean Line. The territory assigned to the New York office includes New England; New York; Pennsylvania, east of Pittsburgh, and Wilmington, Delaware.

Very sincerely,

Miss M. K. Seagrave
Secy. to Mr. Colton

From Hospital to Home

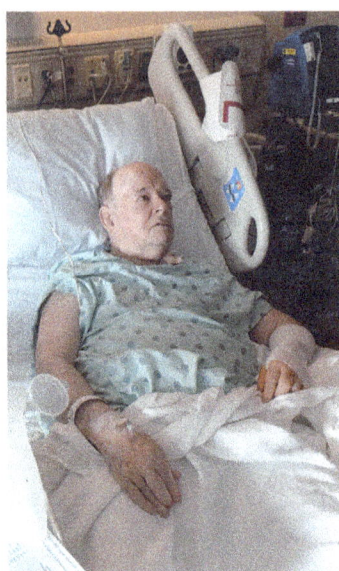

Recovering at Johns Hopkins Hospital after surgery #1. 13 ½ hours.

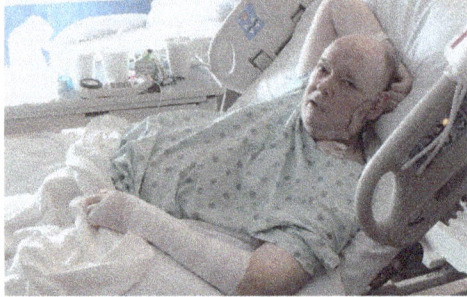

Dr. A. Tufaro and Dr. D. Cooney performed surgery # 1

The nurses surprised me with this beautiful ragdoll kitten, Genevieve, to keep me company. She does a very good job!

Hosting a party for the American Cancer Society. Garden District house was bought in 1984.

Photo Gallery 107

Making good use of new wrought iron handrails, which are now used more than I ever expected.

With Lauren Selden, one of Sherrie's triplets, who came by for a visit. I also love the other two, Elizabeth and Victoria.

Chief nurse Susan Badeaux dispensing morning medication. She has made many trips to Johns Hopkins with me. Besides taking such good care of me we laugh a lot.

108 *No More. No Less.*

The Taryn Möller Nicoll Paintings

Me and artist Taryn M. Nicoll at the unveiling of "Time Out: Tufaro, Cooney, and Colton." The 8' x 6' piece was transported to Baltimore and unveiled in the William H. Welch Medical Library. It was gifted to the Johns Hopkins Department of Plastic and Reconstructive Surgery in the name of my surgeon, Dr. Anthony Tufaro.

Taryn explains her artwork to family, friends and colleagues.

Me standing proudly in front of Taryn's "Time Out: Tufaro, Cooney, and Colton," which was initially shown at the L.S.U. Neuroscience Center of Excellence by its director, Dr. Nicholas Bazan.

110 *No More. No Less.*

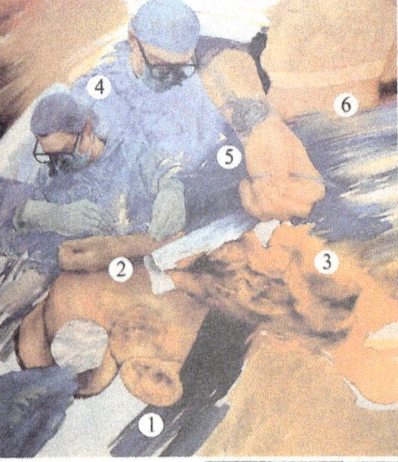

JOHNS HOPKINS
MEDICINE
The Johns Hopkins Department of Plastic and Reconstructive Surgery

"Time Out: Tufaro, Cooney and Colton"
by Taryn Möller Nicoll

This oil painting is the artistic documentation of an epic 13.5 hour surgery that was performed on September 4th, 2014, at Johns Hopkins Hospital, Baltimore MD. It celebrates the bravery of the patient, cancer survivor Mr. Richard C. Colton, Jr., and the heroism of his unparalleled surgeons, Dr. Anthony P. Tufaro, D.D.S., M.D., (associate professor of plastic and reconstructive surgery and associate professor of oncology, Johns Hopkins University School of Medicine) and Dr. Damon S. Cooney, M.D., Ph.D. (assistant professor of plastic and reconstructive surgery, Johns Hopkins University School of Medicine) as personally witnessed by artist Taryn Möller Nicoll.

1. Prior to the first incision, Dr. Tufaro -a world renowned expert in head and neck cancers and craniomaxillofacial trauma and reconstruction- marked the area of skin on Mr. Colton's cheek that would likely be lost during the tumor removal. Dr. Cooney, who specializes in microvascular reconstruction, then traced that linework onto a piece of paper to use as a template for the boundaries of the free flap to be taken from Mr. Colton's arm.

2. Here Dr. Cooney draws the outline for the radial forearm free flap to be taken from Mr. Colton's left arm. Not only is the skin from the forearm transferred to the area of face that was lost to cancer, but the radial artery and vein are attached to the blood vessels of the head as well. The blood supply to and from the flap maintains the supple texture of the 'new' facial skin, which doesn't inhibit speech or swallowing.

3. While Dr. Cooney worked on harvesting the free flap from Mr. Colton's arm, Dr. Tufaro commenced removal of the tumor within Mr. Colton's cheek brought on by squamous cell carcinoma. The remainder of Mr. Colton's parotid gland had to be removed at this time as well. After the tumor was removed, the surgical team worked with their pathology laboratory for hours to test the margins of the surrounding tissues for surviving cancerous cells. At the same time, Dr. Tufaro prepared the area to which Dr. Cooney would attach the blood vessels of the free flap.

4. This area of the painting shows both surgeons working simultaneously, situated towards the top of the composition where they survey every component of each procedure. As Dr. Cooney (middle left of painting) works for five hours to prepare the free flap, Dr. Tufaro (upper middle of painting) not only looks down toward the area of Mr. Colton's face from which he was removing the tumor but oversees the entire thirteen hour surgery. Together, these two experts formed the pioneering team in which Mr. Colton whole-heartedly placed his trust, his health and his life.

5. A skin graft from Mr. Colton's upper thigh was applied to the area from which the free flap was harvested. Here Mr. Colton's hand is shown in a graceful position, loosely holding the tubing from the Vacuum Assisted Closure device that is placed over the graft. This device removes excess fluid, causes increased vascularity and decreases bacterial colonization in order to increase the graft's rate of healing.

6. After the radial artery and vein were attached within the head using microsurgical sutures, the flap was then secured in place using the diagonal 'baseball' stitches seen in the photo above. The results were striking • Mr. Colton's appearance was superb and largely preserved. After a full day of being extensively operated upon, Mr. Colton was taken to the Intensive Care Unit of Johns Hopkins' Weinberg Building.

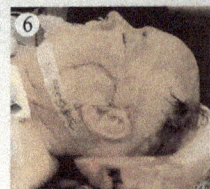
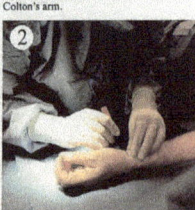

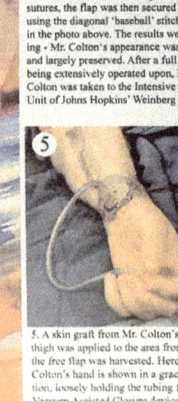
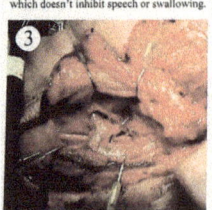

Supporting the Work of Local Artists

Terrance Osborne surprises me with a painting of my dear departed cat Pookie. This portrait lives in my heart and hangs in my hallway.

Me and Terrance Osborne in front of the Fr. Val Ambrose McInnis art piece I commissioned and gifted to the Fr. Val A. McInnis, O.P. Tulane Catholic Center.

I am introduced as the unveiling ceremony begins at the Fr. Val A. McInnis, O.P. Tulane Catholic Center.

Terrance talks about the creative and spiritual inspiration for the painting of Fr. Val A. McInnis.

Talking to the group gathered for the unveiling in the beautiful new building at Tulane University.

Guests at both ends of our little group join me, along with Madelaine Kuns Brushini, Director of Development at Tulane Catholic Center, and Fr. Thomas Schegden, Chaplain of the Tulane Catholic Center, to enjoy this stellar event.

Me with Madelaine Kuns, Director of Development, artist Terrance Osborne, and his mother, Sylvia Osborne, celebrating the gift of Terrance Osborne's painting to the Fr. Val A. McInnis, O.P. Tulane Catholic Center.

Artwork in My House

The first thing you see as you enter my home: Terrance Osborne's original 2018 New Orleans Jazz Festival painting of local Rock and Roll legend Fats Domino with his piano. His familiar pink Cadillac is outside his house in the Lower 9th Ward.

Susan Badeaux and I look at Terrance Osborne's original 2014 New Orleans Jazz Festival painting of the Preservation Hall & The Preservation Hall Jazz Band.

Me, Lauren Selden, Susan Badeaux, and Sherrie Soule study the original diptych painting by Taryn M. Nicoll. This surgery, by Dr. Stephen Metzinger, is the only one for which Taryn was not in the operating room.

Here I am discussing the significance of the replica piece which was painted by Taryn M. Nicoll. The original, "Time Out: Tufaro, Cooney, and Colton," was given to the Johns Hopkins Department of Plastic and Reconstructive Surgery.

Being Honored in Great Company

Leah Chase escorted by her son, Edgar Chase III, at the Southern Dominican Gala. Both Leah and I were honored with the Dominican Province of St. Martin De Porres Award in 2007 presented by Fr. Val McInnis.

Me surprising Leah Chase with a $25,0000 personal contribution check for her continued recovery from the devastating effects of Hurricane Katrina on her family-owned restaurant, Dooky Chase, at the Southern Dominican Gala 2007.

The Leah Chase Gala held Monday April 23, 2012 at the New Orleans Museum of Art

"Cutting Squash," immortalizing the beloved Leah Chase in her kitchen, wearing her proverbial hat. The painting by Gustave Blache III is currently on display at the National Portrait Gallery, Smithsonian Institution.

Leah Chase and myself at The Leah Chase Gala held Monday, April 23, 2012 at the New Orleans Museum of Art. She was honored for her long time influence on our culinary community, her strong civil rights commitment in the 60's and her strong belief of helping the African-American community in their involvement in the arts. The artist Gus Blanche presented 20 original works of her in her restaurant "Dooky Chase". I had the humble experience of introducing her and sponsoring the Exhibit and our Book - a privilege I'm very humbled by. She has entertained three Presidents: Clinton, Bush and Obama.

Leah Chase and I at the New Orleans Museum of Art-Leah Chase Art Exhibit Vernissage Event. This picture and the above caption was used as the front cover of my 2012 Christmas card.

This group picture was taken after my opening ceremony speech at the New Orleans Museum of Art Leah Chase Art Exhibit Vernissage Event. (L to R) Me, Matthew Waldron, Pam Waldron, Judge Dennis Waldron, and Leah Chase.

In My Front Garden

The Lykes propeller that was previously in the lobby of the Lykes Center on Poydras Street in the Central Business District of New Orleans before the company moved to Florida. I made a deal to purchase the propeller for $25,000, and they accepted. It was transported by a flatbed trailer and unloaded into my front yard by a crane. Each lug nut alone weighs 32 lbs.

This driftwood horse sculpture in my front yard was purchased in Saratoga Springs.

This Bronze sculpture by Ed McGowan represents parts of my life: From the top (inner ring) Lykes Brothers flag. Proverbial handshake represents our shipping of AID cargo. Depiction of my house. Religious elements of my life. A straw hat from the long days of summer, racing thoroughbreds which illustrates one of my finish line winners. Baseball bat and NY Yankees insignia represents my love for the game, Henry Moore sculpture—I had the distinct pleasure of visiting him in England. An art palette celebrating my love for fine art. Lykes vessel, a sea barge clipper carrying barges. The first Lykes schooner vessel transported cattle from our Florida farm to our Cuba farm. Replica of my pagoda in Japan. The winding vine represents the human struggle with its beauty and the thorns that one inevitably encounters. The outer ring offers tributes to: Howell Poetry, which is my mother's poetry. Women of the World, my personal collection of paintings from 174 countries. Audubon Stables: for my love of horses. Mowglis, the camp I went to in New Hampshire. Katrina is a cautionary lesson that should never be forgotten.

Birthdays with Family and Friends

Celebrating my 76th Birthday Party at Commander's Palace in the Coliseum Room with many dear and wonderful family and friends.

My recent 77th birthday dinner was also held at Commander's Palace, in their Wine Room. Hoping for many more such events—and birthdays!

My great friend Betsy Becker Laborde is also my personal trainer. She comes to the house weekly, keeping me in shape.

120 *No More. No Less.*

One of my most prized possessions, 1000 Cranes, that a woman named Nina Clark put together and presented to me before last Christmas. She worked at the Four Seasons Hotel in Baltimore where we always stayed before treatments or surgeries. The cranes represent 1000 wishes for good health, longevity, truth and fidelity. Sometimes you receive wonderful gifts that are not expected, and this one belongs in my heart. I can only thank Nina a 1000 times over.

Mom and Dad in their later years at popular Antoine's Restaurant. They especially loved having meals there with the entire family in attendance.

7

A Persistent Adversary, A Continuing Miracle

Baltimore, November 2016

As my cab pulled into the parking lot of Johns Hopkins Hospital, I watched the sky above the Patapsco River. Clouds the color of iron roiled across the city. "Looks like a storm is coming," I told my nurse, Susan, clutching my coat tighter against my chest.

"I'll never get used to the weather up here," she replied, helping me out of the cab after it stopped at the curb. "The wind goes right through you."

"Well let's hope our visits become more infrequent," I said. "Believe me, I'd rather be sitting on my porch in sunny New Orleans."

"At least we'll get to see Dr. Tufaro," she said.

Thankfully, both the heat in Dr. Tufaro's office and his own affable welcome to us were much warmer than the weather outside. I had come to Baltimore to follow up on some standard scans Tufaro had ordered a few weeks prior. There had been no distressing transmissions from up north, so I figured no news was good news.

I figured wrong.

From the moment I sat down in his office, I saw something in Tufaro's demeanor that reminded me of another meeting we'd had together the day between my first and then second surgeries, when he told me my cancer had returned, more aggressively than before. Now I searched his eyes. His expression and posture made my heart sink in my chest. When you are as familiar with doctors and hospitals as I have had to become, you get a sort of sixth sense about these things. You pick up on things others do not. For example, the way a nurse's voice will become hushed as she walks past your room. People not wanting to meet your eye when they have bad news. A nervous grimace on a face right before devastating information is about to be delivered. Right now Tufaro's body language was clearly subdued. Even before he spoke, I felt like a popped balloon. "Richard, you and I have gotten to know each other quite well," he began.

"Well not everyone has seen the inside of my head," I joked, still hoping that Tufaro was not going to say that which I instinctively knew he *was* about to say.

The joke didn't land, deflected by the gravity of the moment and the intensity of Tufaro's concentration. I could see he wanted to deal with the matter at hand and understandably probably wanted to get this over with.

"Okay," I said. "Let's have it. Give it to me straight up."

"Okay. Richard. Here's what the imaging tests show. Your cancer has returned. Aggressively. New tumors have formed around your left jawbone, and in the artery going into your brain."

When Tufaro said the word "jawbone" my hand instinctively reached toward my face, my fingers feeling along my jawline. Strange, I didn't feel any tumors, but nonetheless they were in there, once again throwing my life into chaos. Those growths were like terrorist sleeper cells, hiding just under the surface of society, ready to wreak havoc the moment any sort of guard was let down.

"Right...right," were the only words I was able to croak out.

After a moment of silence, Tufaro continued. "We're limited in terms of treatment options," he said. "We've given you all the radiation we can give you, and these tumors are too large to be intercepted by any new form of chemotherapy. They are already a clear and present danger to your health. In fact, it's sort of a miracle that you're walking around now without intense pain."

"There are many miraculous things about Richard Colton," Susan chimed in.

"Okay then, Doctor T," I said, in what I hoped was a neutral voice and with as much bravado as I could muster. "What are you suggesting?"

"Surgical intervention. We'll have to remove some more of your jaw, and you'll probably lose more facial tissue, but it's the only way I see..."

"...of me surviving," I finished his sentence for him.

"Well...yes."

Susan put her hand on my shoulder. I saw that for some reason she was looking up at the ceiling. I looked at the ceiling too. Unfortunately, there weren't any answers up there.

"Richard, we will need to get the procedure scheduled as quickly as possible," Tufaro said. "Actually, it might be better if you were just admitted directly to Hopkins today, if possible, even if it means you'll miss Thanksgiving. Every day we don't act is a strike against us."

I nodded my assent. What choice did I have? A *third* surgery! Cancer was a persistent devil. I would now have to go through it all again—the confusion of anesthesia, the bright lights of the operating room, the dread Goon Squad. At least I would be with Tufaro. If I had to go under the knife, his hand was the one I wanted holding that instrument.

"Given that this is the third time we'll be performing surgery in the same area, and given the amount of scar tissue the radiation treatments have produced, there will be some heightened risks this time around," Dr. Tufaro had to tell me. "I'll have to be exceedingly careful with how much tissue I remove, and from where," he added, "as you are at an extremely high risk for stroke. Anyone in your condition, and at your age, needs to be aware of these things." "I'm aware," I replied, the full weight of the situation settling into my chest and lodging itself there. This news was an interloper, one that applied the same kind of emotional devastation you might feel after someone broke your heart, or a close friend or family member came to you with some really bad news. Now bad news seemed to be a part of my cellular makeup, swirling around with my cancer cells as well as my healthy ones, always ready to announce itself with a calamitous crash.

"But I'll always keep the promise I made to you, Richard," Tufaro added gently, taking hold of my arm. "I will not let you die on the operating table. I can't promise anything about what the rest of the day will throw at you, but when you're on my table I *will* keep you alive."

I clasped his fingers, giving him a firm handshake. "That is a promise I will hold you to, Anthony Tufaro," I replied.

"I'm a man of my word," was his reply.

Once again Tufaro kept his promise. But his other statement, that he could not protect me all the time, also proved to be true. I had my roughest road yet straight ahead of me.

This journey was one which, in some ways, I was just setting forth on in Baltimore on that cold November day.

I took a deep breath as a boom of thunder echoed from the outside sky. Tufaro went over to his office window and drew the curtain.

"Looks like the rain is about to start," he noted.

"The storm is still out over the river," Susan said. After peering through the curtain, she came over and helped me up from the chair. "If we go now we can get into a cab without getting wet."

With her beside me I walked as steadily and as quickly as I could down the corridor and out to the parking lot, hoping to stay one step ahead of all of the elements that were beyond my control, one step ahead of both the coming downpour and the other force: the one within that also loomed on the horizon, heavy and gray.

* * *

Tufaro scheduled me for surgery two days before Thanksgiving. Since the procedure was so sudden and so close to the holiday, John Carrere, Dennis Waldron and others who had customarily accompanied me were unable to be there. I don't hold it against them. They were spending time with their families, as they should, holding each other close at this important time of the year. Being a bachelor had afforded me a great deal of freedom and enjoyable times over the years. This was a moment when I acutely felt my lifestyle's compromises. Had I married, and had a family, no doubt my wife and children would have abandoned the turkey and trimmings to be by my side. Alas, we all make choices in life. This was a time when I had to live with the realities of mine.

Incredibly, and something for which I will be forever

grateful, someone just as good as family came to the rescue. Taryn picked up my phone call on the first ring. When she understood the situation she said she'd be on the next plane to Baltimore. Even though I had not asked her to do that, she did it. Between her and Susan, I knew, or at least hoped, I could get through this third surgery emotionally. It was going to be up to Tufaro to determine if I could get through this physically.

Once again, as she had previously, Taryn made arrangements to observe this third surgery firsthand and then use her photos and observations as the material for a new painting or series of paintings. Her positive presence, and the addition of an artistic project to my surgery, especially this extremely delicate one, gave me a sense of purpose. With this project, the whole business was about more than just me. In all humility, I did feel that I was contributing in my own way to a work of art that would hopefully live beyond me in impact and longevity. No matter how long I remained kicking around on this earth—of course I hoped that would be a lot longer—the work that Taryn created would continue to artistically portray my struggle with the disease, and my reality as a man.

These positive thoughts kept me going throughout the day, right up until the moment I was wheeled into surgery. Yup, there I was once again, naked under a thin, uncomfortable hospital gown, and once again I was blinded by the lights of the operating room. Still, Tufaro's promise and Taryn's commitment to the artistic end of this journey formed two sets of powerful contracts that gave me the energy and even the eagerness to once again, as the anesthesia mask was placed over my face, count down from one to one hundred, and once again only make it to ten before darkness descended.

* * *

The first thing I remember about waking up from this third and what I hoped would be my last surgery, was the *pain*. It was so fierce that I thought my skin was on fire. I tried to raise my arms to touch my face and see if in fact it was on fire, but my arms were heavy, as if they were two cinder blocks attached to my shoulders. After I managed to make a sort of croaking sound, a nurse came in, hit a button next to my heart monitor, and I quickly felt the warm rush of opiate-induced relief.

I don't remember falling asleep, but I obviously did because when I woke up again I was in a different, less brightly lit room, and Taryn was sitting by my bedside. I could still feel the steadying presence of heavy medication in my veins so, at least for the moment, the pain was manageable. Taryn's sympathetic smile also alleviated some pain, the other, deeper, more nebulous kind that resided closer to my heart than in my bones.

"How did it go?" I asked, hoping for her usual recounting of the events. She was my spy in the operating room, my war correspondent on the front lines. I was eager for her always insightful description.

Taryn's smile became a little sadder. It looked as if she was straining to hold her expression in place. "You have to rest now," she said, not providing me with her usual narrative. "Doctor's orders."

"Am I all right?" I asked.

"You're alive and I'm here," she said. "And guess what?" she added.

"What's that?"

"It's Thanksgiving. We can sit and watch football all day long!"

That was enough for me, at least for the time being. In the coming days though, I would find it hard to get real answers out of *anyone* as to the outcome of the surgery. I kept getting some refrains along the lines of: "Focus on your recovery. You need your strength." I did as told, but of course there was intense curiosity nagging at the corners of my mind.

As it turned out, Taryn had been instructed by Tufaro and the entire medical staff not to overload me with information. I didn't get the *entire* story until nearly two months later. In hindsight, I am grateful to him and to all of them. Had I known the full truth of what had happened during surgery, I most likely would have panicked, and thus been unable to fully focus on my recovery. In fact, I might not have made it out of Johns Hopkins alive.

It wasn't until after I had made a full recovery, had another consultation with Dr. Tufaro, and insisted Taryn tell me every detail, that I was able to piece the story together. I will try to faithfully recount it from the perspectives of both Taryn and Tufaro.

This is what Tufaro told me: that immediately after he opened me up he could tell this surgery was going to be more difficult than the previous two. As he had expected, most of my living tissue was badly scarred from all the radiation I had endured. However, in addition to that hurdle, the tumors were even greater in size than the imaging had shown. The tumor in my jawline came right up to the bone—though thankfully it was not *embedded* in the bone. However, the second tumor was situated in the worst possible place: the artery going directly into my brain.

As Tufaro explained, he knew he had his work cut out for him. Over several hours he carefully resected the right side of my face by removing the entire facial bone down to my jaw, the joint, and part of the jaw bone. It was a difficult operation technically, but thankfully, under his experienced and gifted hands everything did go relatively smoothly.

What Taryn reported was that she was in her usual place, photographing the procedure from just behind the doctors. The mood, she said, was serious but not unusually so. One of the attending surgeons had just bought a new car and the doctors were chatting about it. This may be surprising to you, but even in the midst of intense procedures doctors often chat about mundane things. It keeps them relaxed and helps to relieve pressure. This is similar to how firefighters are able to talk and laugh with their crewmates shortly after pulling people from a burning building. Or, closer to home, why cancer patients make morbid jokes while hooked up to chemotherapy drips. There are times when you just have to deflect from the relentless reality you face in order to deal with those highly challenging moments.

That day, however, there was no deflecting from the reality that had faced Dr. Tufaro in the operating room. While attempting to remove the second tumor, a hole opened on my carotid artery and the situation immediately became life-threatening. Tufaro had no choice but to quickly stitch up the wound, and in so doing abandon any possible removal of the rest of the tumor. In other words he had removed some but had not been able to remove all of it. So it was still lurking there, inches away from my brain, and perhaps inches away from ending my life.

There was nothing he could do. Taryn told me that he looked up from his scalpel and announced to the room: "Frankly, we have to stop—now. I am not going to kill him here on the table, today." Well, for sure he had just kept his promise for a third time.

Tufaro ended the surgery by sending several masses of tissues to pathology and getting me ready to be closed up. Taryn watched him closely as he wrapped everything up. As I was wheeled out of the operating room, Tufaro started to leave very suddenly. Taryn ran down the hall after him. When she caught up with him, he was leaning against a doorway, shaking his head.

"I just wanted to say thank you for doing what you did," Taryn told him.

Tufaro began to speak, but he couldn't seem to finish his sentence.

"You did all you could," she said.

Tufaro again started to reply, then seemed to change his mind, Taryn related. After a moment, he spoke. His tone was serious. "You know," he said. "I have to fly tonight. I have to go see my mother for Thanksgiving."

"I'm sure she will be grateful to see you. I know Richard will be very grateful for what you have done for him," Taryn said, I'm sure in her most soothing tone.

He said: "It's moments like this…" And then he shook his head and left.

Taryn said she didn't pursue him further at that point. She could tell he was too upset.

Hearing this, I was incredibly moved by the intensity of Tufaro's reaction to his not being able to totally heal me. That speaks volumes for the kind of surgeon he is, and the kind of relationship he has with his patients. For him this wasn't just a surgery that didn't turn out the way he thought it would: this is a person he couldn't cure, and it left him deeply troubled. He knew at that point that he couldn't do what he had set out to do. There was much disappointment and pain in that realization, even though, as Taryn said, he *had* done his absolute best—and in fact had done all that anyone could have done.

Taryn stayed in the intensive care unit with me for two more days while I recovered. At that point she had to start making phone calls to the people closest to me to inform them of the situation, even though I didn't yet know all of it myself. She called my sister Elizabeth, my cousin John, and my executive assistant Sherrie. Taryn told me later that she was overwhelmed by the situation, as she was still somewhat in the dark herself about Dr. Tufaro's *plan* for me, going forward.

Of course Dr. Tufaro's plan was what everyone wanted to know, and it was still very obscure. All she knew was that I had a challenging road ahead, and also that she needed to comfort the family. It was a tough moment for her, but as usual she pulled it off beautifully with remarkable grace. She put her faith in Dr. Tufaro and trusted that whatever he communicated next would be the best course of action. He was the expert and she totally deferred to his timing and judgment.

I can feel for how difficult that time was for her. As my friend she must have wanted to tell me what was going on. At the same time, it wasn't her place to go against Dr. Tufaro's wishes. She had to take her cues from him while evading my constant requests for more information.

The day after my surgery, Taryn stayed with me for as long as I was awake. Every moment that I was conscious I was in terrible pain. Thankfully I had an automated control button that I could push every ten minutes or so for relief. With her by my side I made it through that first day. Sad to say, the night was a different story.

I would fall asleep okay, but stir and wake shortly afterwards. Taryn had gone back to her hotel, since her husband Stephen had just arrived from Florida. It was dark and eerie in the intensive care unit; the only sound were the beeps of the heart monitor and the soft pattering of nurses' footsteps up and down the hall. My mind began to race. *What was going to happen to me?* I asked myself. *Why wasn't anyone telling me anything about the surgery?*

A wave of pain rushed through my body and I began to toss around in my bed, trying to locate the medication button. I found it and pushed it, but nothing seemed to happen. *What the hell?* I thought. *I'm going to die here, alone, in this bed.* I began to yell for the nurses. They came in fast and tried to calm me down, telling me that my blood pressure was way out of control, that I had to try to relax. As if it could be that easy. I remembered how Nancy Reagan told drug addicts to "Just say no." Easy to tell me to relax, but at that point it was nearly four in the morning and I was in an absolute panic. I was convinced that I was going to have a heart attack. I kept yelling that I needed Taryn, that I needed her to come to my side *now*. Eventually someone did put me on the phone with her.

Taryn tried to assure me that she had checked, and the hospital staff said there was no major issue, but still I was consumed by fear. "Okay Richard, I'm coming back there right now," she told me. "But I need you to know that everything is okay." To her great credit, she understood that this, while not a true medical emergency, was a sensitive moment. She was on the other end of the line with someone who had just come out of a six hour surgery, was in pain, and was truly concerned for his life.

In a cab on her way over, still on the phone with me, she tried to divert my attention toward something other than my blood pressure or frazzled mindset. "Tell me about all the football games you watched today," she requested. "What were the scores?"

Even in my state of absolute panic I could tell her every game that was played that day, every score, and every outcome. I had just given her the last update by the time she got out of the cab and ran into the hospital.

"I'm downstairs," she told me. "I'll be up in two minutes."

Suddenly I felt I could breathe again. When Taryn entered my room a few minutes later, my blood pressure dropped back down to a safe level. She held my hand and I told her all about the football games again until I fell back into a merciful, drug-induced sleep.

*　*　*

The next day John Carrere came to Baltimore. It was the day after Thanksgiving. Taryn was relieved that a family member was finally present. If anything were to happen he would be able to make decisions on my behalf. When John arrived, Taryn sat him down and went over everything she knew. Now at least my closest family member knew the whole story, even if I didn't. Taryn was relieved to know that John would be there for me for whatever happened. In John's mind, as in hers, the best course of action was to let Dr. Tufaro come up with a game plan. Then we would all follow his lead.

Again, you have to remember that I was in the dark for all of these discussions, and would be for the next several months. So for the next few days in the hospital I was my usual self. When I was awake I wanted to know everything about the surgery, and plied the staff who came into my room with question after question, with the exception of the guy who came to empty the trash—well, maybe not. Hey, maybe *someone* knew something about my condition that was clearly being held from me. "No news is good news" wasn't working. I was desperate to know how the surgery had *really* gone. John and Taryn kept having to repeat: "Dr. Tufaro did everything he could. We'll find out soon what the next steps are."

John shared later that withholding information was very challenging. Like Taryn, he too wanted to be able to tell me everything. But of course he was under orders to say as little as possible. Plus, he wasn't a medical professional, and the last thing he wanted to do was say anything discouraging and deal me a blow that would hinder my recovery. Every single one of my recoveries had taken longer than the one before, and was a little more laborious and strained. Like the others who had my welfare in mind, John wanted me to have all of my power and strength before I had to tackle what came next.

***

New Orleans, December 2016

That period of time was marked by pain—a lot of it. It was like nothing I had ever experienced. It was as if the combined pain of *all* of my surgeries up to that point had released themselves into my body with a vengeance. The pain started the moment I woke up in the morning—visceral, burning, debilitating pain that ran through my face and to a lesser degree my arm like an army of marauding fire ants.

It was the holiday season in New Orleans, which is usually such a warm and comforting time, but I didn't feel like celebrating. When I wasn't in terrible pain I was trapped in a medicated fog from the strong opiates I had been prescribed. I've never been a fan of pain medication. I knew the potential for addiction these drugs carried. But at that point I had no choice: the pain was just too much to bear. During this time I also felt depression slipping back into my consciousness. As I mentioned before, you have to work to keep depression at bay, and there was simply too much on my plate at the moment to adequately defend myself against it. I walked around my house in a daze, waiting on my next appointment with Tufaro, at a loss for what to do until that meeting. Once again I felt like I was slowly slipping under water.

During this difficult time the only bright spot was my local doctor, Charlie Smith. Dr. Smith really became a hero to me for the way he looked after me, and how he was able to help me manage my unprecedented amount of pain. I am not exaggerating when I admit that I called him up all the time, even if it was eleven at night, or later. He was just always there for me. Sometimes when I would call he would be on the golf course, and would talk to me between putts. Sometimes he would be home with his wife Lynn. If Lynn picked up my call she would chat with me as if I were a visitor in her home. They were both so kind to me, and became a sort of lighthouse in the stormy scenario that had become my daily reality.

In all honesty, if it weren't for people like Charlie Smith, I wouldn't have made it through this time. He perfectly provided the warm human touch I needed from another doctor, and gave me his assurances that I could be weaned off these dangerous opiates. He was right: I was able to eventually do so with great success.

I have to remind myself again and again how incredible all of my extensive team of doctors were, and how fortunate I was to enjoy that sort of access that most people battling cancer don't have. I was working with a team that spoke to every one of my needs and truly cared for my well-being. I would not be here today if each and every one of them had not played their unique and purposeful role in my long road to recovery.

***

Baltimore, January 2017

On an unseasonably mild day in January, I sat in Tufaro's office as he finally explained the particulars of my third surgery. John and Taryn were by my side as I received the information they had known for months. It was a lot to take in, but let me say again that in hindsight I am very glad they did not tell me anything until the proper moment. Thinking of my blood pressure in those early moments of recovery, I can just imagine what would have happened if they had told me then that they weren't able to get out all of the tumor. In my condition, with the pain making it difficult to think straight, or get into a positive frame of mind, it would have been devastating. Also, in the time that had passed, Dr. Tufaro had been able to work on a comprehensive plan for my future treatment. But now, as it turned out, that plan included some shocking news: news that even John and Taryn did not know.

"Before we go any further," Tufaro said, "I want to make one thing very clear, Richard. You are no longer a candidate for any sort of surgical intervention."

"No more surgery sounds good to me," I said, my joking manner returning as a small defense mechanism against the massive amount of information I was now finally being given.

"That's not what I mean," Tufaro said, shaking his head. "I'm saying that if the tumor at the base of your skull continues to grow, there will be nothing I can do surgically. You have exhausted this option. Frankly, if I operated on you again I would be breaking my Hippocratic Oath. You would likely not survive the operation, and I have made a promise to you that I would never let that happen."

Another ball of tension built up in my chest. Damn, this cancer was a persistent adversary! It seemed to bounce back from everything we threw at it, like a baseball batter who can get a hit out of any combination of pitches. "Please tell me there is another option," I said hopefully. Now, if ever, was the time for some medical miracle.

"There is," Tufaro replied, and Taryn, John and I all gave an audible sigh of relief. "We aren't quite beat yet. Later today you are going to meet with a colleague of mine. Dr. William Sharfman is one of the best oncologists in the world. He is working with an experimental new drug called Keytruda. It is a monoclonal antibody used to treat patients with unresectable or metastatic melanoma."

"What is that, in normal human speak?" I asked.

"It's basically an immunotherapy treatment. You'll be using your own cells to fight your cancer. From what I've seen the results have been very encouraging."

"And I can meet with him today?"

"Yes. We need to get started as quickly as possible."

I looked over at John and Taryn, who nodded. "Works for me," I said. I stood up and shook Tufaro's hand. "Thank you, doctor," I said from the heart, looking him hard in the eyes. "For your expertise. And keeping your promise."

"Of course, Richard," he said with emotion.

After that momentous consultation, John, Taryn and I went out for lunch. As we walked into the restaurant, I felt the haze I had been struggling through these last two months begin to lift. It seemed that I had an option called *Keytruda!* I was intrigued by this new drug—especially the fact that it was described as a "PD1 inhibitor." When I looked it up on the Johns Hopkins and Cancer.org websites, I discovered what PD stands for, and here are those descriptions:

From the Johns Hopkins website

Researchers at Johns Hopkins Kimmel Cancer Center are leading the way in developing novel immunotherapies called anti-PD-1 and anti-PD-L1 for people with advanced melanomas. The therapies aim not to kill cancer cells directly but to block a pathway that shields tumor cells from immune system components able and poised to fight cancer.

The pathway includes two proteins called programmed death-1 (PD-1), which is expressed on the surface of immune cells, and programmed death ligand-1 (PD-L1), which is expressed on cancer cells. When PD-1 and PD-L1 join together, they form a biochemical "shield" protecting tumor cells from being destroyed by the immune system. Another protein involved in the pathway and also expressed by cells in the immune system, programmed death ligand -2 (PD-L2), was originally discovered by Johns Hopkins investigators in 2001.

"Tumors can co-opt PD-1 to their own advantage to fly below the radar of the immune system," explains Suzanne

Topalian, M.D., director of the melanoma program at Johns Hopkins, and a professor of surgery and oncology. "By using a blocking agent against PD-1, we can interrupt that shield protecting the tumor from immune destruction."

From Cancer.org

An important part of the immune system is its ability to tell between normal cells in the body and those it sees as "foreign." This lets the immune system attack the foreign cells while leaving the normal cells alone. To do this, it uses "checkpoints" – molecules on certain immune cells that need to be activated (or inactivated) to start an immune response.

Cancer cells sometimes find ways to use these checkpoints to avoid being attacked by the immune system. But drugs that target these checkpoints hold a lot of promise as cancer treatments.

PD-1 is a checkpoint protein on immune cells called T cells. It normally acts as a type of "off switch" that helps keep the T cells from attacking other cells in the body. It does this when it attaches to PD-L1, a protein on some normal (and cancer) cells. When PD-1 binds to PD-L1, it basically tells the T cell to leave the other cell alone. Some cancer cells have large amounts of PD-L1, which helps them evade immune attack.

Monoclonal antibodies that target either PD-1 or PD-L1 can block this binding and boost the immune response against cancer cells. These drugs have shown a great deal of promise in treating certain cancers.

Essentially, then, Merck's Keytruda is a blatantly "anti-death" or, to put it another way—a potentially *lifesaving* drug. Yes, yes, yes! For the first time since my surgery I felt a surge of optimism—the energy that only hope can provide. What could have been a very traumatic moment filled with a lot of disappointment suddenly took on a new context. I now had a whole new road that I was about to travel down. I wanted to get rolling.

* * *

In response to this third and final surgery, Taryn created two remarkable oil paintings and a series of black and white watercolor studies. I now have three of the watercolors in my house. She related that for her this surgery had been much more difficult to represent on canvas than the previous two. For one thing, there wasn't the same feeling of triumph she felt in the earlier work. In these artworks she had focused more on anatomical close ups, and in the final paintings there are many more areas where you can see the doctor's fingers and gloves navigating and moving around the inside of my face.

Taryn later admitted to me that when she had painted these she had been filled with sadness and dread, feeling that the cancer was coming out ahead. As someone who cares for me, she was deeply upset by what was happening at this point in the treatment. For the first time in my cancer journey the doctors were not in charge: these uncontrollable anatomical elements seemed to be taking over. When you look at these two new oil paintings you understand the gravity of my situation. They are gritty paintings. But it was a gritty time in my life. I think she represented it perfectly.

Lunch was over. It was time to meet Dr. Sharfman and find out if he held the "key" to my survival.

* * *

8

Recovery's Long Road: Becoming Stronger In The Broken Places

Baltimore, January 2017

It was thirty degrees outside. Heavy winds whipping over the East Harbor made the sparse waterfront look even more miserably frigid. Fortunately I was indoors, comfortably settled into a leather-backed chair at The Bygone, a gleaming restaurant on the twenty-ninth floor of the Four Seasons Hotel. Watching the streets below through a floor-to-ceiling window, I saw lines of men on the docks loading crates into shipping containers, while out on the Patapsco River a few boats slowly chugged past them. Along the riverbank promenade a few scattered families wandered toward the National Aquarium.

I turned my gaze downwards to watch a woman outside the hotel. She shivered as she smoked a cigarette. Her condensed breath mingled with the smoke emanating from her mouth, indistinguishable from one another. Perhaps it was my state of mind, but at that moment the working men, the scurrying families, the lone woman—everyone I watched—seemed to me like they'd rather be somewhere else. I knew that I certainly would. I was tired of the cold, tired of an endless carousel of doctors, consultations, surgeries, and changing predictions as to how long I was going to live. I would much rather have been back in New Orleans. I watched the woman finish her cigarette, hail a cab, and depart for somewhere else. She had the right idea.

My dour mood was a rare one. In fact, I had been in better spirits only a few hours prior, when Dr. Tufaro told me I was going to be meeting the new oncologist he had described. Today that specialist, Dr. Sharfman, was going to start me on Merck's new immunology drug called Keytruda. I had taken Susan out to lunch, where we talked excitedly about this new drug, which the doctor had also used for a select few patients with the same type of cancer; a drug which could potentially save my life.

However, after lunch a dark feeling settled over me, as this thought popped into my head: *This new drug might save my life, but how many times will my life still need saving?* By now I had already been saved three times by Dr. Tufaro. I had been told with certainty that I was no longer a candidate for additional surgical intervention, chemotherapy, or radiation. This Keytruda and prayer were all I had left. How many more chances was the universe going to give me? Was I cashing in too heavily on my contract with God? Was I doing enough good deeds in the world and fulfilling my end of the contract to warrant the continued miracle of my existence?

After practically pacing a hole in the carpet of my hotel room I—on impulse, without telling anyone where I was going—found my way to the elevator bank, got into the lift, and hit the button for the top floor. When the doors *clinged* open the first thing I saw in front of me was a sign that said *The Bygone*.

Well, that's almost too on the nose, I thought to myself. With my increasingly bleak prospects, if there were ever a place to mull over one's mortality it just might be a restaurant called The Bygone. Though I had just had lunch, I sat down anyway and ordered myself a crab cocktail. I wanted something to remind me of home, and something to inject a glimmer of pizzazz into this drab day.

I don't know exactly how long I sat there, while a pile of crab with chive Hollandaise sauce sat untouched in front of me. I just knew I needed that time to look out over Baltimore's Harbor again. I'd felt a kinship with the tiny figures I had seen earlier, which steeled me somewhat against the battle to come. I thought: *If those people can brave the cold to work their blue collar dock jobs, spend time with their families, or enjoy a final cigarette before heading off on an unknown journey, than surely I can muster up a little more strength to fight cancer.*

A light touch on my arm broke me away from my ruminations. My ever-vigilant nurse was standing over me, an element of worry etched on her face. "You scared me," Susan said. "Please don't run off like that."

"But you have such a talent for finding me," I deflected.

"What's brought you all the way up here?" she asked, noticing the uneaten food on the table.

"Oh, you know—thinking."

"This is a good place for that. But we've got Sharfman in 30 minutes."

I was still lost in thought. "Sharfman..." I repeated the name as if it were a distant acquaintance I was trying to recall.

"Yes, Dr. Sharfman. I think it's just about the only meeting in the world you can't miss, Richard. So let's make it," she urged with a smile.

Suddenly the stupor that had invaded my mind like a deep mist rolled back, and in its stead I had a moment of terrifying clarity. Gripping Susan's arm, I said, "I think this is my last chance." From the instant look of empathy on her face, I could tell Susan thought so too. There was no denying the reality facing us. Being the remarkable person she is, she did what she always does, softening the edges of my neediness by offering her warm if unspoken support. Taking the hand that gripped hers, she used it to pull me up out of my chair, and continued to hold my hand as we walked over to the bank of elevators, on our way to face yet another uncertain outcome.

* * *

As we entered Dr. Sharfman's office the sound of a bell suddenly rang out with a triumphant peel. A tall, beaming man was holding the glass bell. I watched as he rung it once more, a huge smile on his face. Then he replaced the bell on the reception desk and then shook hands with a shorter man who was standing next to him. That man was wearing a white coat and had a little skull cap on his head. The jolly bell-ringer, still smiling broadly, strode confidently towards the door. A few other people seated in the waiting room gave him an enthusiastic round of applause as he left.

"Are we in the right place?" I asked Susan with uncertainty.

"It says 'Dr. William Sharfman' on the door," Susan replied.

Hearing his name, the shorter man in the white coat turned toward us and extended his hand to me. "You must be Richard Colton," he said. "I'm Bill Sharfman."

How had he known it was me? I wondered. Then I remembered that not too many people have a face that looks like mine. Fortunately, I sometimes forget that I look different.

"Pleased to meet you." I replied. "Did that patient win a prize?"

"If you consider being cancer-free a prize," Sharfman said.

"I do indeed," I enthused.

"Our patients ring that bell on their last day of treatment," he continued to explain. "That sweet sound means they are in full remission."

At his words a shimmer of hope ran through me. If that patient had been saved by this drug, it must really work. Maybe my *last* chance had a decent chance!

"Let's get some privacy so we can talk about your treatment options," Sharfman said, leading me into an examination room. It looked exactly like the hundreds of examination rooms I had been subjected to over the past few years. I looked around for a bell in here, sighting only a jar of tongue depressors. The bell seemed far away now. Reality was much closer.

Susan and I sat down, with Sharfman seating himself across from us. Adjusting himself in his chair, he tapped a pencil against my chart. "Your medical history is unusual," he said. "I'm very good friends with your surgeon, Dr. Tufaro. Had I not heard the details directly from him, I might have been skeptical. But here we are..."

"Well here is *most* of me, at least," I interjected, trying for levity. It's one of the ways I cope with tense situations.

"It's remarkable that *any* of you is here," the doctor countered. "I'm in charge of the Medical Oncology department here at Hopkins and let me tell you, you are lucky you ended up with Tufaro. However, it seems that even his capable hands were not quite enough to beat this thing."

"And you have something that might?" I said, my voice filled with hope.

"I think so. See, Mr. Colton, your case is rare because of two things: The type of cancer you have, and the location of it. As you know, you have squamous cell cancer of the skin, and it has metastasized to your neck and to the jaw on the left side of your face. What's much more common is head and neck cancer that spreads to the skin, not skin cancer that spreads to the head and neck. Your type of cancer usually requires a small operation where the surgeon cuts it out, and that is the end of it. That is what happens in ninety-nine percent of the cases. It's unusual that your cancer has progressed the way it has. This tells me it is very aggressive."

"When do I get the *good* news?" I said. Susan laughed in spite of herself, and Sharfman cracked a little smile.

"Not quite yet," he said. "One challenge we face is that there is no approved medical therapy for recurrent squamous cell skin cancer. There have never been enough patients to do studies."

"Well I've always been a bit of a one-off," I said.

Ignoring my self-deprecating comment, Sharfman continued. "I am very involved in immunotherapy for the treatment of cancer," he said. "My focus is melanoma. There have been great advances in immunotherapy for melanoma. Lucky for you, it turns out there are compelling reasons to believe that the squamous cells in skin cancer will also respond to immunotherapy."

"I was confused. I thought cancer was treated with radiation and chemo," I asked.

"Immunotherapy is just what the name indicates: therapy that turns on the body's own defenses," he instructed. "It's a way of helping the body to recognize cancer and eradicate it. This is something that I have long thought is the *right* way to treat cancer. I have never believed that chemotherapy was going to be the answer. To me, and many other physicians and medical researchers, it makes more sense to 'turn on' the immune system to eradicate a tumor. This way you are also not letting those toxic cocktails kill off healthy cells, as they most often do. Immunotherapy is a more natural way."

"So with immunotherapy you have the good soldiers fighting for you internally," Susan interjected.

"That's right," Sharfman agreed, smiling at her and then turning back to me. "Starting about seven years ago, these types of immunotherapy drugs began coming into the market. They are what we call 'checkpoint inhibitors.' Not to get too technical, but in simple terms, we all have brakes in our immune system that prevent that protective system from going overboard. If we didn't have these brakes, we'd all get an autoimmune disease such as Lupus or something else. But if we turn off these brakes for a bit, we can fight cancer very aggressively. Bottom line, immunotherapy works by turning off the brakes in our immune systems."

"Fascinating," I said, sincerely.

"The first breakthroughs in skin cancer were with the drugs called Ipilimumab and Nivolumab and then Pembrolizumab. Merck, the renowned pharmaceutical company, puts Pembrolizumab out under the brand name Keytruda." Sharfman continued. "It has worked for kinds of cancer similar to what you have."

"Why didn't any other doctors suggest we try this on Richard sooner?" Susan asked, always my defender.

"The medical community has just recently become aware that it could work in skin cancer like yours that had either just formed tumors, or had formed tumors that had already spread," Sharfman replied.

"So there's no real data on whether this will work?" I asked.

"There are anecdotal reports of these drugs working on patients with your type of cancer," he noted. "And there are clinical trials going on now, but these take time. There's no data back yet."

"Oh," I said.

"I am happy to say that I was able to petition Merck to try out your case with Keytruda," he related. "This may help save lives."

"I hope it helps save *my* life," I said.

"That's the idea," Sharfman agreed with a reassuring smile. "You're not going to be getting any placebo. It will be the real drug. Honestly, I think it's your best chance."

I was a little nervous, but what other options did I have? "Okay," I said. "I'm game."

"I knew you were a fighter," Sharfman said warmly. "Here's how it works: Keytruda is taken intravenously every three weeks. So you'll have to fly up here to get your treatments."

Hmm, no rest for the weary. There was still going to be a lot of extensive commuting in my immediate future, but at least I seemed to *have* a future.

No matter, I had made my peace with it. I shook Dr. Sharfman's hand and stood up to leave his office.

"Well," I said. "Here's to my someday ringing that bell."

***

Baltimore, January 2018

After she struck the needles into my arm, the nurse made sure the IV was running properly, then she put the TV on and left me to my own devices. I watched the liquid dose of

Keytruda slowly drain into my veins. Unlike chemotherapy, there was no pain, and no horrible nausea flooding my system. Quite the opposite—every time I took a dosage of that treatment I felt myself grow stronger. I actually enjoyed watching the clear substance go into my body. It was as if I was being given some life-giving elixir that had been previously unavailable from me.

That day's Keytruda treatment marked my twelfth, taken over a period of about eleven months. As it turned out, Dr. Sharfman's plan seemed like nothing less than a miracle. My latest CT scan showed that all my remaining tumors had shrunk dramatically. Dr. Sharfman said he was exceedingly confident about my prognosis, which had now changed from dire to near remission. He admitted that if Keytruda had not been introduced into my life, I most likely would not have made it this far. The effect of immunotherapy was not unique to me: many patients with different kinds of cancers *were* going into long-lasting remission.

Nonetheless, the doctor wanted us to remain cautiously optimistic. We were not home free yet, as there still was no long term data for squamous cell skin cancer with these newer therapies. In truth, I was sort of a guinea pig. He did assure me there was more clinical research available for melanoma, a somewhat similar skin cancer. He reported personally putting forty-plus percent of people with metastatic melanoma into remission for multiple years with Keytruda. Forty percent may not seem like a high percentage, but it was significantly higher than my previous chances of long-term survival, which had hovered right around *nil.*

What was perhaps most remarkable about Keytruda, and why I considered it a true miracle, was how it had gotten rid of my pain. As I related in the previous chapter, the pain I had been dealing with after my third surgery was truly horrific. It was so debilitating that I had stopped being able to live my normal life and was fast becoming a shell of myself. Unthinkably for me, I would sometimes not take lunch at Joey K's for weeks. But after just one treatment with Keytruda the pain had significantly receded. After my second month of treatment my pain was *entirely* gone. As anyone knows who has struggled with cancer-related pain, or chronic pain from any source, the relief of said pain is truly life-changing. You get back a whole area of existence that had been closed off to you when, understandably, all you could focus on *was* your pain.

The way I talk about Keytruda you'd think I was being paid by the company. Just the opposite is true. While the treatments were free, as I was part of a limited study, had I not been able to afford the many trips up to Johns Hopkins, or been able to stay in comfort at the Four Seasons Hotel, I would probably not be alive today. I deeply appreciated all of my advantages, and knew that, as part of my contract with God, I had to keep paying it forward and make a meaningful difference in the world with the extra time I was being given. I had started that process by helping Taryn create art, and done some other things, but I knew I needed to expand my "doing good" much further. I was still pondering what form that should take.

When this bag of Keytruda was empty, signaling that this treatment was finished, the nurse removed the IV and Dr. Sharfman came in to see me. He told me exactly what I had been hoping to hear: my latest CT scans and MRIs showed even further remission of the tumors. I would only need about six more months of treatment. At that endpoint he hoped all of the cancer would be fully banished from my body—ideally never to return. Needless to say, my heart swelled with joy.

"So?" I asked. "After this final treatment it will be my time to ring that bell?"

"Oh," Sharfman said, suddenly looking melancholy. "I was actually going to tell you. We had the bell removed from the office."

"Why?" I asked. A feeling of sadness washed over me. For a year I had been waiting to ring that bell. In my mind it signified the sound of victory.

"Well Richard, you are one of the lucky ones. Not everyone gets to ring the bell you know. In fact, most don't."

"I see."

"Imagine if I told you today that your cancer had returned and had given you, say, a five percent chance of making it in life for another year. Then you stepped out into the waiting room and saw someone ringing the bell. How would that make you feel?"

"It might make me feel happy for someone else who was going to make it. Solidarity in the ongoing battle with cancer, and all that."

Dr. Sharfman shook his head. "Or it might make your own prospects seem that much more grim. It might discourage you and make you want to quit fighting."

"I'll never quit fighting."

"I know *you* won't, Richard. That's one of the many things I admire about you. And, thanks to Keytruda, your fight is going to last a whole lot longer."

When I boarded the plane for my return to New Orleans the next morning, I was full of excitement. I was going back to my old life, comforted by the knowledge that I could now fully enjoy my daily life without a massive albatross metaphorically tethered to me. I "rang the bell" in my own mind, knowing the best of times was yet to come.

What I didn't know then, was that something *was* definitely coming, and soon. Alas, it was not something I would ever call "the best of times."

* * *

New Orleans, Winter 2018

Back in New Orleans I did slip into my old life. I went to the racetrack, saw entertainment programs at Sacred Heart, and ate lunch each day at Joey K's. One day, toward the end of January, I was sitting and reading the paper: I had to resort to the paper when the Yankees weren't on, since spring training didn't start for a few more months. An item caught my eye, a detailed article about the current flu season. Apparently it was one of the worst in recent times, with senior citizens the most impacted, as they always are. I made a mental note to get a flu shot as, come to think of it, I had been feeling slight shivers even in my warm home. I dismissed it, as I often did with little changes. Once you go through the pain of cancer and all its attendant drama, other maladies tend to not seem as threatening.

That day I had a horse running on the New Orleans Fair Grounds Racetrack. Just then my phone rang. It was Judge Dennis Waldron, asking if I would like him to join me at the track that afternoon. Eager to see him, I immediately accepted, and went to dress. While putting on my coat, I glanced in the mirror and noticed that my face seemed a little pale, but I just splashed some water on it as I heard my doorbell chime.

By the time we got to the track I was feeling quite groggy,

but racing always puts me in a good mood, and as we were seated in the box I felt the old joy crash over me. Here was everything I loved in life: old friends, the smell of horses and fresh-cut grass, the process of putting in my betting slips and the hope that those I wagered on turned out to be winners. Yet, on the first few runs I was having trouble concentrating. Everything seemed slightly out of focus, as if I was watching the proceedings on a malfunctioning television where the picture kept blurring.

"You okay, Richard?" Dennis asked, ever perceptive. "You seem a bit wobbly."

"Sure, sure," I mumbled.

At that point, because I think he was concerned for my well-being, Dennis called Matthew and told him to come to the Fair Grounds. Matthew arrived, and we all watched another couple of races together.

I was still feeling out of sorts and, at one point, got up to use the bathroom. As I stood, I swayed slightly, and then saw the floor rush up towards me. As I began to fall I felt Matthew's strong arms supporting me, with his dad on the other side, helping to prop me up.

"It's fine," I said. "Just a little…"

I couldn't even finish my sentence. A thick fog was creeping into my head. I felt fully underwater now, submerged.

"Let's go," said Matthew, snapping into coach-like command. "Dad, let's carry him to the car."

Quick as a lick, they helped me out of the track and into the car. Everything began to move fast now, like a montage of images. "Where are we going?" I asked groggily.

"Touro Infirmary," the Judge said. "You're burning up, Richard."

"We'll be there in no time," Matthew promised, punching the gas. Out the window pieces of New Orleans turned like images on a screen. I had no connection to them. I just wanted to close my eyes.

All of a sudden I was on a gurney, being wheeled somewhere by two doctors, one dressed in white and one in green. Matthew was running along at my side, speaking rapidly to a doctor about what had just happened. "I'd say he's got an extreme case of influenza," I heard a doctor say. "It's all over the city right now. We have to act fast."

I felt Matthew squeeze my hand. Then a mask was placed over my face. Then darkness.

∗ ∗ ∗

I do not remember much of anything that transpired over the next forty-eight hours. All of it has been related back to me. The doctors had immediately determined that not only had I caught this "super flu," I also had a case of walking pneumonia. As a result, my lungs were quickly filling up with fluid. It sounds strange, but many people go around with this, not realizing they have it until it's too late. Jim Henson, the creator of The Muppets, had also ignored some symptoms, and then died suddenly from walking pneumonia, as have many others.

The physicians who cared for me had no choice but to immediately perform a tracheal intubation—a fancy way of saying that they put a breathing tube down my throat to keep me alive. To be able to do this they had to put me under, using an extremely strong drug you may have heard of called Propofol. This basically put me in a sort of controlled coma for forty-eight hours or so. Propofol, one of the drugs—if not the main one—that killed Michael Jackson, commonly causes short-term memory loss, which certainly explains my actions over the next few days.

As I said, I remember very little of this, but apparently when I finally woke up I acted quite strange. As Matthew Waldron put it, I was "acting like a raving drunk." As I do not drink very much I find this quite funny, but my situation was very serious. I did not realize how sick I had been until much later. The truth is that, once again, but for different reasons, I had come very close to death. At the time I was certainly in no state to receive such information, but the coma-inducing dose of Propofol they had given me had lasting after-effects over the next several days.

Waking up, I found myself extremely confused and almost immediately began to hallucinate. It was as if I was dreaming while awake. Everywhere I looked I saw strange colors and lights. For some reason I even began to hallucinate that my nurse Kristine was riding on a llama, while leading a large pack of llamas. I think I hallucinated this because her young son loves llamas, and my subconscious chose this moment to bring this out. She was leading this massive pack of llamas through town and then down to the racetrack, where she rode them around and around as if they were competing in the Kentucky Derby. Then she led them out of the racetrack and began to make her way toward a giant train in the distance—obviously also a figment of my drugged-up mind. I saw that the train was full of senators and congressmen: people who would certainly disapprove of her roving clan of llamas.

"Don't, Kristine!" I cried aloud. "You'll be arrested for your llamas!"

The real Kristine, who was by my bedside, obviously didn't have a clue as to what I was talking about. "Huh?" she asked.

"Please, please they are going to take you and all the llamas to jail."

It took her quite a while to calm me down and convince me that there were no llamas in the hospital room. She also tried to assure me that she had no idea how to ride a llama in the first place.

Another time I began to imagine that I was walking around the halls of the hospital, and then down to the gift shop. Suddenly I decided I did not want to be in the gift shop any more. I had to be out of that gift shop immediately! I turned to another nurse who was with me then, named Judith, who, in my hallucination, was also somehow in the gift shop. I demanded that she take me back to my room.

"But Richard, we *are* in your room."

"Nonsense! I want to go back to my room."

"But... we are here. Just look around you."

Real Judith was making no sense. I was getting really angry. "Take me back to my room or you are fired!"

She again repeated that we were in my room. So I fired her on the spot.

When I woke up the next morning, I was a little more lucid. It felt like I had a bad hangover. Now it was my main nurse, Susan, who was sitting near my bed.

"Guess what, Susan?" I started.

"What?" she asked.

"I fired Judith last night."

She got confused and asked me why I fired her.

"She would not let me go back to my room."

"But you've been in your room the whole time."

"No, I was in the gift shop. She wouldn't let me go back up to my room."

"Richard, I don't even think this hospital *has* a gift shop. I saw that Judith was upset last night. Now I know why."

"So I wasn't downstairs?"

"No! Look, you are hooked up to an IV. How would you have gotten that out of your arm?"

"Oh," I said, "I guess I owe Judith an apology."

Susan and I agreed that from now on I would not do any more hiring or firing while under the influence of extremely strong pharmaceuticals. Still, I wasn't quite out of the woods when it came to Propofol hallucinations. The drug was so powerful that it stayed in my system for at least another twenty-four hours, producing results that, in retrospect, seem mildly hilarious. On another evening, I awoke—or at least thought I awoke, in the hospital pharmacy downstairs, my mind and body being in very different states of consciousness. The pharmacy seemed otherworldly. The pills on the shelves glowed menacingly as I groped my way through the aisles toward the pharmacy desk. I didn't want to try to fill a prescription—I wanted to ask the pharmacists for directions back to my room. Fear had gripped me like a vice and my only objective was to get back to my room, where I would be safe.

When I reached the pharmacy desk, my confusion was further compounded. The white coat clad technicians were filling prescriptions, but they were also, for some utterly incomprehensible reason, selling rotisserie chickens. There was a large roasting rack behind the counter, which the pharmacists were tending like trained chefs. Patients would walk up, get their prescription filled, and also receive a piping hot platter of chicken. I could even smell the chicken—smoky and full of Cajun spices. The room swirled around me, flavors and fear filling my senses in a way that was totally overwhelming.

I turned to my right, and lo and behold, there was my nurse Kristine standing by my side. Where had she been this entire time? She had just appeared, like a ghost out of my memory. The reality of the situation, of course, was that Kristine was the *only* real thing that I was seeing. The rest was just a bad "trip," as those experienced with drug-related street terminology might describe it. Having never done any hallucination drugs before, I was unable to tell what was real and what was a figment of my imagination induced by the psychotropic drug in my system.

I clutched at Kristine, demanding that I be taken back to my room.

"But, Richard, we *are* in your room," she implored me, with a look on her face like she was seeing a movie she had viewed many times before.

It took a great deal of convincing on her part, but she was finally able to calm me down. Once I slept a bit I realized I *was* in my hospital room, and not trapped in some chicken-shack-pharmacy nightmare.

Luckily, my agreement with Susan from the day before held, and I didn't fire Kristine on the spot. Thank goodness I didn't! I don't know how she would have reacted if I kept blaming her for holding me captive in the worlds to which Propofol transported me. Thankfully, though, this was the last of these encounters, and I hoped my last brush with Propofol. I certainly don't enjoy the confusion that such strong drugs inflict. And I certainly can't imagine any scenario where I'd need to get chicken and medication at the same location!

* * *

A few days later, which happened to be Super Bowl Sunday, Matthew Waldron came to visit me in the hospital. As I've told you before, Matthew is an extremely perceptive young man. He noticed that I was slurring my speech and appeared to be generally out of it—not even able to follow the game. Before, this had been ascribed to the effects of the Propofol, but by now those effects had worn off.

The doctors were called in, and it was determined that, coming out of intubation, I had suffered a small stroke. While in my state of serious duress a blood vessel going to my brain had narrowed, one that went to the area of the brain which controls speech and language. I ended up spending thirty-four days in the hospital—the longest stay of my life.

My cancer battle was a long difficult journey, but this was the single most dangerous sudden illness I had ever encountered. A super flu, walking pneumonia, and then a stroke, all in one go. It is truly a miracle that I didn't die. I suspect the fact that Keytruda had supercharged my immune system had something to do with my ability to survive this medical tsunami.

That I was in New Orleans may have also aided my recovery. There I was, surrounded by supportive friends, with my home base only a few blocks away. I hate hospital food, and once I was well enough, Sherrie—who as I explained earlier, in addition to helping run my life as my executive assistant, also worked as a part-time waitress at my favorite restaurant—snuck in lunches from Joey K's. She was my double agent, bringing me not only daily food but also daily gossip from outside the hospital walls.

Matthew and Dennis Waldron also visited me often, and Susan was always by my side. I can honestly say that I would not have made it through this ordeal without the help of my wonderful friends and nurses.

I was released from Touro on February 28th, 2018. Once again God had upheld His end of the contract. Now it was time for me to fully uphold my end.

* * *

9

A Contract With God Fulfilled

New Orleans, April 2019

My bags were packed and I sat waiting beside the front door. In just a few hours I would be on a flight to Baltimore for what I hoped would be my last immunotherapy treatment. As I related in the previous chapter, over the course of the last year I had undergone thirteen of these treatments, the combined force of which had thankfully sent my cancer into remission. Barring something unexpected seen on my final CAT scan, Dr. Sharfman planned to suspend the treatments after this visit.

As I waited for the car to take me to the airport, I thought about his bell. Had he not removed it from his office I might have finally gotten to ring it. No matter, I told myself—I will buy one when I return home. Actually, my plan was to place the bell on a table under one of Taryn's oil paintings depicting the surgeries I'd undergone, and ring that bell anytime I pleased. I could imagine the sound, each sweet *ding* synonymous with the word "alive."

If everything went well in Baltimore, I was going to come through this nine-year battle scarred but still breathing; still able to enjoy the things that made life worth living, and worth fighting for. It seemed that God was going to hold up His end of the pact I had made with Him after receiving my initial diagnosis. At the outset my odds of survival had frankly been dismal, yet here I was. Every heartbeat, every breath, was an act of defiance against death.

I still had some time before I needed to leave for the airport, so I decided to use the time to meditate on the paintings in my front parlor. The vague uneasiness that usually occurred around travel days had settled over me, and art always has a wonderfully settling effect on my nerves.

Walking down the hall from my bedroom to the parlor I caught a glimpse of my reflection in the glass of a framed painting. It was early morning and the light seemed to gleam and illuminate the crevices of my facial scars. My hand shot up to my left cheek—to the place where my intact jawline had once been. I felt the space—the weight of what wasn't there. I had survived, but I would never be the same, physically, emotionally, or spiritually. A large part of my appearance had been permanently altered, vanished into the ether of cancer. My face would always be misshapen and battered, but the acceptance of this realization brought me no pain. And really why should it? My appearance was a testament to my experience of the disease—and, for now at least—my victorious emergence.

This reminds me of this famous passage from the Velveteen Rabbit by Margery Williams that I read as a young boy: *'It doesn't happen all at once,' said the Skin Horse. 'You become. It takes a long time. That's why it doesn't happen often to people who break easily, or have sharp edges, or who have to be carefully kept. Generally, by the time you are Real, most of your hair has been loved off, and your eyes drop out and you get loose in the joints and very shabby. But these things don't matter at all, because once you are Real you can't be ugly, except to people who don't understand.*

Today, my altered face is as much a part of me as every other part of my aging body with its many changes. But appearance is one thing and "identity" is another. We are all marked by life in one way or another, and ideally will bear our changes proudly—or at least without feeling less than. In my situation I chose to retain my identity, scars and all, and be the same, only, as fully as possible, an even better man. Cancer is a disease that creeps into every aspect of one's daily life. There is not and never will be a going back to my former life, even if the disease remains in remission forever. And this goes far beyond my altered appearance. For one thing, I have years of physical therapy ahead of me. There also will always be the looming threat of recurrence. I have prepared myself for that reality, and try to not keep it top of mind, hoping I will have plenty of time in front of me to continue to serve, as a force for good, as I had promised my Creator.

Of course, there is no denying that I have become a truly different person then when I began this journey. My relationship with my family and friends, with my doctors and nurses, with my city, with art, with my faith, and most of all with myself, have all been modified in a significant fashion. In my situation I chose to retain my identity, scars and all, and be the same, only, as fully as possible, an even better man.

Each of these aspects of my life is now aligned with my ongoing, challenging battle with cancer. Confronted by near-certain death, I had undergone many long moments of doubt, and had ultimately found my way to a stronger place.

Turning away from my reflection, I walked over to my favorite armchair, sat down and looked out my big picture window at the stately Southern oak trees that line my block.

On their branches there still hung streamers and beads, remnants from last month's Mardi Gras. This year's celebration had been, as it always is, a riotous few days. Although I didn't partake in the festivities to the full extent, as I had in my earlier days, I still managed to enjoy myself.

This year's Mardi Gras made me fall even more deeply in love with my adopted hometown. This city has an eccentric quality that can't be replicated anywhere else on earth. New Orleans culture understands and rewards uniqueness more than any other place. I believe that's why I fit in so well here. As I once said to Dr. Sharfman, I'm somewhat of a one-off myself. Plus, I have never felt judged here for being myself, even when that *outward* self changed radically.

My experience with cancer has made me appreciate New Orleans on a much more personal level. It made me realize that beyond the old lanterns, or cracked sidewalks, or crawfish boils, or beignets, the people that live here are what makes this city great. The way that all my friends have rallied around me when I needed them most has convinced me that I chose the right place to live out my life. When you get cancer people show you who they really are. Some people run *from* you. Others run *towards* you. For those who do stay steadfast, you want to make sure you have your arms open to embrace them.

John Carrere was one of those who had run towards me. His support, not to mention his driving skills, have been most valuable for my many trips to Johns Hopkins. He may be a cousin but I have always seen him as a brother. This experience had deepened our bond in ways I couldn't have fathomed. I don't think he expected to sit by my hospital bedside for hours on end, but that's just what he did. When I needed him, he was always there for me.

The same goes for Ernie Carrere. The beauty of my friendship with Ernie is that it has been one of the very few things in my life that didn't change after my diagnosis. Ernie and I have always had the kind of relationship where we can pick right up where we left off, no matter whether it's been three days or three years since we last saw each other. If you're lucky you have similar relationships, be it with friends or family members, who often these days may not live close by.

Some people have treated me differently after my surgeries, as if I were someone to be pitied. Never Ernie. That's the monk in him. He understands how to treat everyone, not just me, because he's very much in touch with his spiritual nature. To tell you the truth, I think he understands God's mysterious ways better than I do.

I had last seen Ernie at Judge Dennis Waldron's birthday party. The judge's birthday fell a few days after the end of Mardi Gras. We used the occasion to gather some old friends together and tell stories we had all heard a million times, but still laugh at. Matthew Waldron was there, fresh off officiating a basketball tournament. His career was continuing to climb, and with each passing day he seemed to gain a greater sense of his place in the world. He reminded me of myself at his age, and I knew I would always help him in any way I could. Matty was part of my Agreement with God—he had aided me in my time of need, and I would help him find his way through the world. Of course he was doing a pretty damn fine job of it already on his own.

That day at Joey K's, it made me smile to see Matthew and his father together, blowing out the candles on the judge's birthday cake. The two of them had probably saved my life that afternoon at the racetrack when they acted as a makeshift ambulance crew. I felt eternally grateful to them for that. They have remained stalwart friends throughout this whole process. Matthew has motivated me, Dennis has counseled me, and both of them have supported me.

My family has also supported me. Although living on the West Coast, notably San Francisco and its surrounding areas, my sisters have shown their urgent concern and provided constant and loving support. I deliberately did not make Elizabeth and Keenan fully aware of the ultimate crisis that faced me due to the inoperable tumor on my carotid artery. Their support from a distance was sufficient: I was grateful that they did not have to directly suffer the peril of encroaching death with me.

I have to say that I couldn't have made it without my nurses and aides. In the current schedule my night-shift nurses, Judith and Angela, arrive after they have put in full days at their other jobs. Angela often works evening shifts at Joey K's. I can't imagine how these ladies do it! Their faithfulness and devotion are truly humbling.

It's clear why Dr. Smith ordered around-the-clock help for me. Taking the full complement of pills and other medications I'm required to be take daily has its dangers. Without the nurses I could very easily overlook some of my meds; worse, I could overdose. My daily routine is now automatic, with specific pills variously scheduled throughout the day and night. Still, I've often had to ask the nurses if I have already taken one certain pill or another. Thankfully, the nurses keep a record. They know far better than I what I need to take when, keeping me on time and on track.

There is even more to this. Initially, Dr. Smith had mandated the nurses to monitor and manage postoperative pain.

As I described earlier, there were times when my pain was "off the charts," persisting at intolerable levels. Dr. Smith was available day and night to advise interim measures to stave off these horrific pains until prescribed medicines could be reassessed, then administered anew in a timely and warranted fashion.

However, certain aspects of my surgeries had also left me with the increased possibility of a stroke, so it was urgent that I have professional eyes monitoring my condition continuously. As it turned out, Dr. Smith's judgment in this regard proved prescient. Kristine and Susan share the twelve-hour day shifts. Each has saved me at crucial moments. At one point Kristine recognized the incipient signs of a stroke and got me to Touro Infirmary Hospital before there was significant damage. In another instance Susan recognized a serious condition when one of my legs turned bright red. She brought me right to Dr. Smith, who determined that I had a staph infection of the leg. Without Susan's practiced and professional eye, that infection, left untreated, could possibly have led to sepsis, with fatal results.

The importance of the nurses became even more apparent when I stopped driving, which really does give you a significant loss of freedom. My nurses are always able to bring me to all of my doctors' appointments and to my lunches and dinners.

Susan Badeaux has been with me nearly three years, and, as my chief or executive nurse, maintains an ordered schedule of the nurses and a calendar of my various doctors' appointments, while serving in many other capacities. Since I have not been driving for some time, Susan and Kristine, and on occasion one of the other nurses, will pick up prescriptions at the pharmacy or make necessary grocery runs. In fact, along with my executive assistant, Sherrie Soule, they all help keep the entire household well-stocked with whatever is needed, and functioning smoothly.

All the nurses have contributed to a wonderful family atmosphere and lifted my spirits. Susan in particular has proven to be simply indispensable. I really couldn't get along without her. Susan has traveled to Baltimore and Johns Hopkins with me for the numerous Keytruda treatments. Taryn has been wonderful in her operations "reportage." She has become a very close confidant during my entire process, thanks in no small part to her insightful discussions with me concerning what happened during my surgeries. Susan and my cousin John have both also served as my "eyes and ears" during countless medical consultations following operations, and then throughout the numerous immunotherapy procedures. As a nurse, Susan of course can understand the medical wherewithal better than a lay person. Most importantly, Susan knows when and how to ask questions, always in my best interests, which is a comfort and reassurance that we are in full compliance with our team of physicians.

Waiting for the car to take me to the airport before that game-changing trip, which turned out to be my final Keytruda infusion, I thought about friends I no longer get to talk to—at least, in the worldly sense. This included my cousin Bronson, who, as I described earlier, had died of cancer on Christmas Eve 2016, and many other cherished friends and relatives. I like to believe they are enjoying Heaven and cheering me on from the other side. It's comforting to think that's what happens to these kinds of good people!

While waiting, my gaze also shifted to a painting hanging

near the front of the parlor: a depiction of Christ by the famous artist Henry Moore. In this painting Moore has Christ embracing the cross rather than being nailed to it. It's almost as if Christ is reaching out towards the pain, eager to accept humanity's sins. It's an active portrayal of sacrifice that reminds me to continuously make efforts towards greater spiritual development and good works, as I promised God.

I have tried to make good on my end in many ways. Through my cancer journey I have come to realize that one of the most important things I can do with my time on earth is to help support cancer research. After all, the development of a drug like Keytruda was the reason I was still able to draw breath. To this end, I had set up an arrangement with Dr. Sharfman that will help fund his ongoing and very important research into better and better immunotherapy drugs. I also am helping to fund Dr. Tufaro's equally valuable cancer-related research. I believe immunotherapy drugs are the future of cancer treatment, and that work both of these doctors are doing is invaluable.

My artistic relationship with Taryn was also part of fulfilling my end of the spiritual contract. Being the subject, and a benefactor, of her artistic career has given both of us purpose at critical times in my treatment. Beyond that specific working partnership, I had also thought of other ways to support the arts. For one thing, I continue to support the work of New Orleans artist Terrance Osborne in his gallery on Magazine Street. I have also donated to the creation of an arts building for my old prep school, The Gunnery, which is set to be completed in April of 2020. I fully intend to be present on opening night for the first show they perform there.

A decade after my initial grim diagnosis, I was still alive.

God had certainly done his part, and with these efforts I had tried to fulfill mine. I knew though, that beyond these efforts, I wanted to do more, especially within the context of art. I reached out to Taryn, and told her that I wanted to use art as a means of helping an underrepresented community. She connected me to Afghan artist and educator Rahraw Omarza. He needed support for his Center for Contemporary Art Afghanistan (CCAA), an art school in Kabul. Despite them being halfway around the world, I became involved in the school's operations. Besides donating money, we sent them critically needed art supplies and arranged transportation to get students to and from the school safely.

This venture culminated in August 2018 with an exhibit of work created by students age 6 to 18 titled "Views From a Distance: Contemporary Afghanistan Through the Eyes of Children." The collection is about Afghanistan, a country we hear about all the time through news media, largely due to America's involvement in a war there. I wasn't able to attend the opening because of my health, but the students sent me many drawings, filled with hopes and aspirations, and the sights and sounds of their native Afghanistan. It gave me great joy to see them. The children were very keen on exploring their life, and reflecting on their war-torn country, while sharing their hopes for the future. Some of the pieces dealt with difficult themes. But, just as many people view the art Taryn and I created as difficult, it's all part of the human condition. The beauty of art, even when dealing with delicate or controversial subjects, gives us a window into our common bonds as humans.

I looked at my watch—it was time to hit the road, and I had done enough reminiscing for one day. This easy chair would be waiting for me when I returned. I had business to attend to in Baltimore: namely a chapter of my life that I could hopefully close out for good.

***

Baltimore, March 2019

In the waiting room of Dr. Sharfman's office, I nervously fidgeted with my handkerchief while I waited for him. I had just finished my Keytruda treatment, a process I was more than used to after the previous twenty-five sessions.

I know it sounds strange to have mixed feelings about getting a clean bill of health, but my eager anticipation was also tinged with anxiety, since I did expect this to be my last treatment. I had grown reliant on the drug—with good reason, as it was literally my lifeline. After my hospitalization at Touro in January of 2018, I had stopped taking Keytruda for several months. The pneumonia and various other health issues I was being treated for made it impossible for me to travel. Consequently, a small amount of skin cancer *had* returned. Fortunately the damage was detected early, and the cancerous areas were removed by my long-time dermatologist, Dr. Coller Ochsner. She has always monitored my health on an extremely meticulous level, even way before this last trip, and now gave me a rather serious warning.

"I hope you stay on Keytruda forever," she told me. "That is my personal opinion. I hadn't seen a skin cancer on you since you started Keytruda. You go off it for a couple of months or so, and you break out with skin cancers again."

That assessment had been given over a year prior to this potentially final session, but you can see why I was conflicted. On the one hand, the end of my course of treatments seemed to be a bright light at the end of this long and arduous tunnel. Yet, I could be making a fatal mistake. In that moment, as I so often did, I prayed for guidance. "Show me what to do, God," I said out loud, since no one was in the immediate vicinity. Normally, I ask God for help in silence. Prayer helps me let go of the things I cannot control, and after saying that, a sense of calm washed over me. I find that when you put your faith in something higher, and believe that everything will turn out in accordance with God's plan for you, it does. Suddenly I knew what I had to do. Just as I had put all my faith in God, I would put all my faith in Dr. Sharfman. He was the Keytruda expert, and had saved my life. I resolved to trust him completely.

At that moment there was the doctor, walking through the door, with a smile on his face, which made my heart quicken. I wanted to shout at him: *Tell me! Tell me! Am I going to be okay?* But I held my tongue. Today was in his hands.

"Richard, how was your treatment today?" Sharfman asked, seating himself across from me.

"Same as ever," I replied, hoping he would get to the good news quickly.

"I'm going to miss seeing you all the time," Sharfman said, his smile breaking out even wider.

"Do you mean..."

"Your CAT scan is clean. I see no reason to continue treatment beyond today."

Now that this moment was here I could hardly believe it. For a good part of the last decade every aspect of my life had revolved around fighting this disease. A huge part of me cried out in relief, while another part remained a bit skeptical. Was it possible? Was I really in total remission? What if, the minute I stopped Keytruda, the disease came back with a vengeance?

I inhaled deeply and let faith take over. I would trust my good doctor, and *all* my good doctors. Most of all, I would trust that God was watching out for me, so that I could do more good in the world.

"Of course you'll need to be monitored and have regular CAT scans," Dr. Sharfman was saying. "But I'm extremely encouraged by what I'm seeing. Let's just say that if I still had a bell in my office, you would be able to ring it today."

"I've been waiting a long time to hear you say those words."

"Well, today is the day."

We shook hands. My heart was filled with gratitude toward this man. There is little in life that gives you more joy than being truly thankful for your continuing health, especially when the alternative is as seemingly inevitable as mine was.

* * *

New Orleans, April 2019

Getting off the airplane from Baltimore, the first place I went to, as you may have already guessed, was Joey K's. Frankly, I could think of no better place to celebrate my clean bill of health. It was my place of comfort, where my usual table would be waiting for me, just as it always was.

When I walked in Sherrie was running the ship. She winked at me and started fixing me an iced tea with two sweeteners shaken into it, like a martini. Every member of the wait staff knows my drink order—a small gesture that means a lot to me. It makes me feel at home, as if I'm having a drink on my front porch.

I ordered the roast turkey with mashed potatoes and macaroni and cheese, no stuffing, and settled down to my meal. The restaurant was packed, as it usually is, but I caught sight of a familiar face moving toward me. Frank, a man I have known for years, was also a cancer survivor. In his case it was prostate. As he made his way to me between the tables, I watched him move slowly. His left hand and forearm were encased in a thick black leather glove. He was in construction and had lost his hand in an accident. I noticed that he was looking a bit down. His disease had obviously taken a toll on him, but last I heard he'd been doing well.

Frank reached my table and we exchanged hellos. I gestured for him to sit so we could do a catch up. He sat, then stared directly into my eyes, communicating silently. One thing about cancer, as I've said before, is that you develop a connection with other survivors. They know what you are going through. Many times they are the *only* ones who can truly instantly connect with you on that level.

"I got some good news yesterday," I said at once. Then I told him about the drug and how, finally, as of today, I was off it for good. "I'm glad for your good news!" he responded.

After a pause, he said, "I've got some *bad* news," adding a small rueful laugh.

"Bad, eh?" I commiserated.

"Yup. Damn thing came back."

"Frank, like what I just told you about me, there are always skirmishes. You just never know when the war could be over, and you could be the winner. Hang in there, buddy."

"You too." With that he smiled, stood back up, and moved away from the table. When he got to the front door, he turned and gave me a small wave goodbye.

A while later Susan picked me and my suitcase up from

Joey K's, and we drove home. As she went inside I lingered in my front garden. As I walked around the yard I touched the giant horse made out of woven branches, a symbol of my love of horses and horseracing. Then I went to stand in front of the enormous golden propeller that once graced a Lykes family ship. Deep in thought, I drifted over to the large round sculpture that sits near my fence. This huge mass of dark bronze is one of my most treasured artistic possessions. It contains images of all the important things in my life. Looking at it always fills me with a dual sense of nostalgia and purpose. The images include the Lykes company flag, flying high above two hands clasped together to represent a trade agreement. There was a dashing horse, flying to the finish line. There was a pious nun of Sacred Heart with the Holy Cross behind her, her hands raised in prayer. There was a mighty freighter ship, forging its way through squally seas. There was a painter's easel, ready to create a masterpiece. There was the baseball emblem of my favorites, the good ole Yankees. There was my mother's name, and my father's. There was also a logo for Joey K's, and one for my other favorite restaurant, Commander's Palace.

As I stood in the yard, feeling the warmth of the sun on my damaged but still serviceable face, and on my scarred body, also still in working order, these reminders of the life I had lived made me wonder about the life I *would* live from this day forward. Hopefully, this deadly enemy, this cancer, will stay quiet and respectful, allowing me to live out my life and do my work for years to come. If it returns, I will battle on with Keytruda, or whatever new weapons are available. If I lose—and in the end we all go back to our heavenly source—I will leave this world with deep gratitude for the extended time I have been given.

It is true, too, that some lingering aspects of this long battle will remain with me for the rest of my days. I have the scars to prove it, literally. My entire appearance has changed radically, along with the way I eat, exercise, and even get around town. I haven't driven a car in several years, and don't foresee that particular skill entering back into my repertoire. I tire much more easily than I used to, and there are lingering medical complications from the many surgeries I've had over the years.

My dental situation is one of those complications—my teeth and gums often cause me extreme nerve pain that cannot be alleviated through surgery. If I have something as simple as a cavity, or a tooth that needs to be pulled, all of which is common for men of my age, it will be a significant operation that will need to be done in a hospital. Most people don't think about things like that; now I'm forced to. The lasting impact of my surgeries and radiation make just continuing to exist a complicated and sometimes strenuous task.

But here I am. And I am happy to be here. In the end cancer has *not* won. How can it, when I now have a new appreciation of every moment of every day? And when, at the same time, as paradoxical as this may sound, I have completely lost my fear of death, knowing that God is watching out for me. I have also been so fortunate to be surrounded by such supportive friends and family, with my talented and caring physicians, caregivers and care *receivers*. Those who allow me to help them, or help them help others is also a gift—to me.

The credo that sums up my attitude towards the challenges

and blessings of this entire ordeal is something I once told Dr. Tufaro. I said that "I am what I am. No more. No less." Those words contain a world of utter self-acceptance. It has been a long journey in a fast-moving train, and right now we have reached a wonderful destination. I hope to stay here—in this positive state of mind, this positive state of health, and this remarkable state of grace—for a very long time. And that is what I wish for you. Now, please excuse me: I have a little bell to ring. And more to do. I know God is watching.

* * *

Treatments with Merck's PD 1 Inhibitor 'Keytruda'

- 2/17/2017
- 3/13/2017
- 4/3/17
- 4/24/17
- 5/15/17
- 6/12/17
- 7/3/17
- 7/24/17
- 8/14/17
- 9/15/17
- 9/25/17
- 10/16/17
- 11/6/17
- 12/19/17
- 1/10/18
- 6/13/2018
- 7/5/2018
- 7/26/2018
- 8/28/2018
- 9/25/2018
- 10/16/2018
- 11/6/2018
- 11/27/2018
- 12/18/2018
- 1/8/2019
- 3/12/2019 — Last Keytruda Treatment. Will continue to see Dr. Sharfman for CT Scans every three months as he continues to monitor my status.

Interviews with Key Members of My Medical Team and Friends

Dr. Charles Smith

Interviewed May 10, 2018
Internal Medicine

My chart goes back to 2009. That is when this computer started, I think it was longer. I think he was my patient long before that. I was his internal medicine doctor for years before all of this skin cancer. He has been diabetic at least ten years. If you go back to 2010, he was diabetic, on antidepressants, cholesterol medicine. He's always been pretty healthy; he just had some issues like we all do. He has had high blood pressure, diabetes, prostate effects his urination, shingles, kidney cysts...so it's a lot. It depends on what you think healthy means.

It's not surprising for someone in his middle sixties to have some of the illnesses. Some were genetic. I don't think he has ever had an excessive lifestyle. It was more genetics and getting older. He did have a tiny stroke in his early sixties.

He has always been very compliant with coming to the doctors. Until we got these nurses working for him full time he had some trouble keeping straight when to take his pills and that kind of stuff. He has really done better with things since they took over. He is a lifelong bachelor and I think he would just lose track of some of this stuff.

So when they took over, it was kind of when he got into cancer treatments, it made it a lot easier for us to treat his diabetes, high blood pressure. Over the last few years he has had a lot of really serious things other than cancer. He had to get a pacemaker put in, he had a stroke, he had pneumonia which was pretty severe. He looks remarkably good considering all he has gone through. And he has had a remarkable spirit his whole life. He had his seventy-fifth birthday party last fall and I really likened him to one of these 19th Century British men who really try to be good at everything. He is involved in charity, business, supporting education, sports teams, and he is very involved with these paintings. I think he really thinks things through and sees them in his own way. He just doesn't follow the crowd in the way he deals with things. Like having this book done and having his story told. That is not something I would have ever thought of doing. I think it is remarkable.

Taryn is very talented as well. So he is good at attracting talented people around him and doing things.

I would say he is recovering from his recent infection. He also has a pretty weak heart muscle. He is recovering from the infections and he probably has a radiation-induced antiopathy on one of the blood vessels in his brain. This is what the neurologist thought, that it is radiation-induced and the blood vessel is irritated. That has caused a blockage in the blood vessel. So when your systolic blood pressure, that is the top number, is below 150 he does not speak as well and he is not as sharp mentally. When you get his blood pressure above 150 and push through that blockage, he is much sharper.

He was 148 yesterday. So here is the tricky thing. Since his heart muscle is weak we would like to get him a beta blocker to protect his heart from the sympathetic nervous system. When a heart muscle is weak, the body tries to stimulate is to pump harder. In the short-term that is good but in the long term it actually wears the heart out faster.

So you try and put a beta blocker on the patient to protect the heart from the sympathetic nervous system. Then you would use a drug which blocks angio tension and that makes it easier for the heart to pump. It's like taking a resistance away so the heart can pump better. So from a cardiac standpoint we'd like him on those two drugs but they would lower his blood pressure to a point where he couldn't talk. I don't know if it would affect Keytruda per se but the Keytruda may start to affect his adrenal glands a little bit. We are monitoring that. We just got a test back yesterday and it isn't as bad as we thought it might be.

Yes, it is very complex. You might say he is looking much better. But if he had a major stoke at some point or went into bad heart failure…anything like that could happen. So we see him once or twice a week in our office.

I think he is unique in that he thinks of projects, works on them and then follows through to complete them.

I think he is a very caring person. He has tried to help a lot of people out when they have started businesses. I think he is charitable. I think he is very well rounded. He can speak well on a lot of different subjects. That is basically who he is. He keeps going despite all this cancer stuff. He is doing the paintings, writing a book, doing charity stuff.

I think with Dick I try and be really positive. I do know there have been times when his spirit was off and he was down. I do think of all the stuff he has survived and how remarkable his spirit is. I will comment on that and I think it raises his spirits. I think he is aware that he has been really sick and close to death. He kind of puts one foot in front of the other every day. It crosses all of our minds when we reach a certain age.

I think he is different to me in the sense that he has a lot of different conditions. I talk to him nearly every day. When he was in the pain period, I was talking to him four or five times a day. It is interesting: he was on a lot of opiates for a while. He came off of them no sweat once the pain went away. It was pretty remarkable to see.

* * *

Dr. Coller Ochsner

Interviewed April 29, 2018
Dermatologist

Dick has been a patient of mine since 1999. He has very fair skin and has spent a lot of time in the sun. Typically we were destroying pre-cancerous lesions and through the years taking off cancerous spots. He had a couple of aggressive ones before 2010 that had to be removed by a Mohs surgeon. In 2010 he had a very aggressive one that started out on his forehead.

He was diagnosed with skin cancer in 2012, but he actually had skin cancer before that. He had multiple skin cancers and pre-cancers that were being removed. The biopsy date is October 29th, 2010. He had a couple of severe cancers in 2010. It was biopsied and was called squamous cell—poorly invasive, poorly differentiated. When you get a cancer that is well differentiated, it's a good sign. That means it has still has some of the microscopic features of normal skin. When it is poorly differentiated that is a bad sign. That means it has none of the features of normal skin tissue and is very aggressive. Poorly differentiated malignancies have a higher likelihood to invade other structures and metastasize to lymph nodes. So the biopsy showed a squamous cell carcinoma, invasive and poorly differentiated on the scalp and the forehead.

On the pathology notes it says, "The tumor involves the base of the specimen, angiolymphatic invasion is not identified" and they didn't know if this was possibly metastatic in origin. Meaning that they didn't know where it really came from. It may not have come from the skin. But they are saying they can't tell if it started here or somewhere else. At that point he was sent to a million doctors. He was sent to Dr. Simoneaux, a Mohs surgeon. A Mohs surgeon is a dermatologist who treats superficial skin cancers. He was also sent to Dr. Seiler, an oncologist. He is the first oncologist that I sent him to. He went to multiple doctors after that and he was the first oncologist.

Dr. Paul Spring was after Dr. Milton Seiler. Dr. Paul Spring is actually a surgical oncologist. Dr. Seiler doesn't do the surgery, but he does the investigation. He did a CT scan of the head and neck that showed numerous cervical lymph nodes, with no evidence of metastatic spread; no mass was seen. A singular, mediastinal node in the upper limits—that is a node in the chest. Numerous non-obstructive cortical cysts, stable linear calcifications. None of this was very impressive.

It was a single mediastinal lymph node in the upper limits of normal. You have nodes in your chest. None of them appear obviously metastatic. When he was going through all of that obviously he was not seeing me because they were in the process of getting it all under control. There were no more skin worries as much as chasing this cancer.

In March 2011, I saw him back. He had shingles and he had multiple pre-cancerous lesions on the rest of his exposed body; we were taking care of that. He started coming pretty regularly after that to stay on top of his skin cancer. The lesions were on his face mostly and his scalp and arms. These were just pre-cancers. Before he had this bad one he had multiple skin pre-cancers that were removed.

There are many kinds of cancers of the skin. Basal cell is common, squamous cell is the second most common and more aggressive than basal. Melanoma is the third most common and way more aggressive than squamous cell carcinoma. But he happened to get a really aggressive squamous cell. It is acting like melanoma for sure and is just as bad as melanoma at this point.

He's doing immunotherapy with Dr. Sharfman. And he is doing awesome on it. Since he has been on Keytruda I rarely find any skin cancers anymore and maybe a few pre-cancers. This is amazing because he had accelerated to the point where I was seeing him every three weeks at some point. Since he has been on Keytruda—let me get the chart—remember he had all those problems and his last Keytruda appointment was 4/17/18 and he had not had a treatment since January of 2018—for about three months because he had pneumonia and the eye infection.

I also saw him in early March this year and he had a new squamous cell for the first time in so long. It was removed on March 8th by Dr. Keith Leblanc, another nodes surgeon. It shows that when he got off the Keytruda all that sun damage he has is starting to break down into cancers again. So he really needs to get back on the Keytruda. I hope he does it forever. That is my personal opinion. I hadn't seen a skin cancer since he started Keytruda and he gets off of it for a couple of months and breaks out with skin cancers. So that tells me what else is happening with that metastatic cancer. It does show it is working. It shows it is working beautifully because once he was off of it three months he had a new skin cancer. Squamous cell happened on his left temple. It did not show the aggressiveness of the one in 2010.

I think he is amazing and I think God willing if he stays on this drug he can beat it. It just shows you how well it is helping. He is quite unusual. He is so down to earth. He actually learned how to make the most of his situation.

We all learn from our fears in life and he's been pretty challenged.

He's been very generous in supporting many charities. Very philanthropic.

He keeps his sense of humor going. He's maintained his sense of humor throughout his ordeal.

* * *

Dr. Stephen Metzinger
Interviewed June 1, 2018
Plastic Surgeon

Richard Colton developed a lump behind his left ear, kind of down on his neck. He went to see an ENT. That doctor thought it was just a boil, so he lanced it in the office. That was a mistake. In fact, it was cancer—specifically a necrotic lymph node. I didn't see the lesion so I can't really speak on how it was missed. Mr. Colton had undergone what is called a PET CT Scan for metabolically active tumors, and the result was negative. So I think that's why the ENT thought it couldn't possibly be cancer. He lanced it in the office and then packed it. Ten days later Mr. Colton comes into my office because the wound was infected and not healing. We got a biopsy and then I referred him to the local Oncologist, Paul Spring. The cultures came back positive, as poorly differentiated metastatic cancer and a staph infection.

When he came in to our offices, we did a complete head and neck exam and found two lesions. Not only did he have the thing behind his ear, I felt a mass in his cheek which I believed was also metastatic. It was on the inside; you couldn't see it but you could feel it. He had cancer in the lymph nodes and an infection. The lymph nodes had become enlarged by the spread of cancer or by the infection. They did the fine needle to see if the cause was the cancer or the infection. That test wasn't conclusive so you have to assume cancer was the cause until proven otherwise.

The whole left side of his neck was involved. From under the jaw bone, in the neck, behind the ear, all the way down to the clavicle and in the posterior neck. He then had different lymph nodes taken out of different parts of the neck. In all a total of forty-four were removed. Of those forty-four, seven of them were positive for metastatic squamous cell carcinoma.

As of now, he cannot have any more radiation. Between his original radiation, the short-term chemo he had and the follow-up INRT he had over twelve thousand Raz. That is a ton of radiation. Arbitux is chemo—just one drug, three doses two weeks apart. They do it as a radiation sensitizer to try and make the radiation more effective.

He was okay for a year and then in July 2000 he developed a lesion on the opposite side. It appeared to be a skin cancer and they weren't sure if it was related to the other location or not. The reason to do the Mohs procedure is to make sure you have clear margins and to try and spare tissue when you are taking it out. In other words, the plan is to get the cancer out but leave the normal tissue behind. Dr. Simoneaux took out so much that I had to do another flap closure. Now he has two sides involved. So again he needed radiation. Because of what happened the first time we really didn't want to take any chances. To complicate matters, his only good eye is on that right side so we had to protect that eye.

The cancer was originally diagnosed on that side by his primary dermatologist, Dr. Coller Ochsner. She built a special shield for him and did the IMRT. They were of course very careful. He has had a total of three radiations on both sides of his body, which is amazing for a human being.

So now we were at March 6th and he was with me again. I did multiple frozen sections followed by a radical resection of his left cheek. I did a cervical facial advancement flap. We cut out all of the skin of his cheek and used some access from his neck to cover the cheek. He had asked if, while I was in there, I could remove some scar tissue, so I did that for him. There was scar tissue around the nerve from previous surgery and radiation. The idea was to try and get his face to work again. He did get some return of function but his face was never as good as had been prior to the radiation. On March 17th, some weeks later, in come the results: ulcerative squamous cell carcinoma with all margins clear, meaning the tumor had been completely resected. No residual disease. This was good news: we got it all.

In April, May, June, July, his life went back to normal. He had almost four months of relief. Then he complained of left sided TMJ pain. He underwent MRI, CT scan, and PET scan: they revealed that this is metastatic and was in the bend of the carotid artery. The thing that Ochsner biopsied was down by his jaw line: this was more by his cheek bone, a completely different area.

Anthony Tufaro and I were residents together in plastic surgery at John Hopkins. I knew that he had trained and done Oncology at Sloan Kettering. He is one of the best head and neck guys in the world so I sent him off there. We had all tried and it kept coming back in different places. The whole area needed to be removed. This was the thirteen-hour surgery. In that surgery with Dr. Tufaro was a plastic surgeon colleague, Dr. Cooney. He did a tissue transfer to close the hole. He took fat from his forearm. It's easier and provides bigger vessels.

In December of 2014 that year he returned to my office for a follow up after his surgery. At that point he had multiple issues. He had been referred to Crane rehab for physical strengthening and speech therapy. Because Dr. Tufaro had removed a lot of the facial nerve, which works the musculature of the lips and cheek, his speech was altered and he had to learn to overcome that. The physical strengthening was for his whole body and face. We got PT to work on his overall conditioning, and then we had them do speech therapy and mobility of his neck and jaw. He was having difficulty eating as well. Dr. Moses Oreaga is an ENT specializing in vertigo. He was having some dizziness so we also sent Richard to him.

At the point he had another PET scan done and it showed a lesion on the inside of the left sided cheek, deep underneath, where the temporal lobe of the brain is. It appeared to be engaged in the bone. So now for the fourth time he is sent back to

Dr. Tufaro—who went in and took out everything. They took off half his face. The problem was while he was doing it they found that his carotid artery was encased with tumor and they couldn't get it out. So they took out what they could and stopped. That is when they decided to treat him with Keytruda.

A year later he has a heart attack and pneumonia. His immune system is a bit diminished and also we had one of the most horrible flu seasons in years.

I have been practicing 32 years. This patient's tumors were without a doubt one of the most aggressive tumors I have ever seen, if not the most. His being fair skinned is a factor, maybe from an earlier time when people didn't slather on protective creams. He was also in Japan for a number of years and I am sure that affected him as well. He was in the shipping business and always outdoors. I am stunned that he has lived as long as he has with his faculties together and just getting on with living his life. He is a great patient and a great man. I think he is one of the grittiest human beings I have ever had known. He has been through a lot but he maintains his dignity and is kind and generous. I am telling you he is a gritty, gritty guy and a good guy. He has good friends and family support. He continues to do good in the community, particularly with the arts. He has done great things. He helps a lot of people. He is a fighter. Keytruda was experimental at the time and he is now a year out. He is doing great with it and it seems to be shrinking the tumor.

* * *

Dr. Anthony Tufaro

Interviewed May 10, 2018
Plastic Surgeon

Richard had treatment for his original skin cancer in New Orleans for a cutaneous malignancy. He had the surgery and radiation. His skin cancer progressed to the point where it left the side of his face and went in to lymph nodes in the gland right in front of his ear, the parotid salivary gland. I wasn't involved at the time so I don't know if this surgery was one hundred percent effective. Then he got radiation again. By the time he got to me, his facial nerve was already involved with tumor, which is a problem. The facial nerve is the one that animates your face. When you meet him, you can see that the left side of his face does not move. Pretty much from the beginning that was a poor prognostic indicator—predictive of a poor outcome. The problem is once the tumor has proven to be aggressive enough to metastasize, leave its primary site to go into lymph nodes, and invade something like a nerve that tells you about the biology of that individual tumor.

When he came to me, he was already pretty far along. He had already had surgery and radiation and actually a surgeon I know in New Orleans told him to come see me. Stephen Metzinger is a very dear personal friend. He and I trained together at Hopkins. Stephen's practice is now mostly cosmetic surgery. He had seen Richard early on. Once it sort of got out of control he sent him up to me. I told Richard he needed a bigger operation and I didn't think he could be radiated again.

I have a complicated background. I am Board certified as an Oral and Maxilloacial surgeon. I went to Dental school initially. I practiced as an oral surgeon for about six years. Then I went back to Medical School. I came to John Hopkins to train and did a few years of general surgery. Then I trained as a plastic surgeon at Hopkins. Then I went to a place in New York City—to

Memorial Sloan Kettering Cancer Center—as a surgical oncologist specializing in head and neck surgery. So I have two hats on. One as a reconstructive surgeon for my plastic surgery training and the other is a surgical oncologist, getting tumors out. Sometimes I just wore one hat and took a tumor out. For some of Richard's stuff I wore both hats.

I got one of my partners, Dr. Damon Cooney, to take a piece of his forearm and use it to fill in the gap from the tissue I had taken away. I removed the tumor and he reconstructed the defect, with tissue from the arm. It is called a "free tissue transfer," meaning we take skin that had been on his arm with a vein and artery attached; we attach that to an artery and vein in his neck so you are putting a piece of living tissue in there. An artery and vein. That worked well. He was good for a period of time. I kept imaging him. He called me after a period of time because he was having a lot of pain right in front of his ear. I imaged him and the tumor had recurred. We took him back a couple of days before Thanksgiving and I actually took out the bone to his jaw, the joint and part of the jaw bone on that side. They were all compromised. The tumor came right up to the bone, though not in the bone. There was tumor on the artery going into his brain.

In peeling it off I saw that everything was scarred from radiation and the previous surgery. There was a hole on the carotid artery I had to fix. I said quite frankly that I was not going to kill him there on the table that day. With a guy his age you don't mess around with the carotid artery going into the brain or he could have a stroke or something like that.

To avoid that, I put two stitches in the artery to stop the bleeding but I knew I didn't clean the entire tumor. I couldn't. I told him we have one thing left and let's see if some of the newer targeted therapy treatments for cancer can work for you.

I sent him to Dr. William Sharfman and he started him on medication and in short order his pain went away. At some point he didn't care as much about the cancer as about the pain. Understandably, he was not functional with the pain which was extremely unrelenting. He was living off of pain pills. A few weeks after starting treatment he didn't have any more pain!

The problem is he has had a lot of radiation so it is difficult to get a wound to heal on Richard. The depression where we took his artery out is less unsightly than the fact that the left side of his face doesn't move. That is the first thing you notice. He talks normally. I think the Keytruda medications, PD-1 inhibitors, are a miracle. Richard was very lucky so far that he has responded early to the drug.

He is going to start Keytruda again. The lesion on his forehead is just a superficial skin thing that they can take off. The guy down there took it off and Richard got a bad infection from it in his eye. That is not uncommon in radiated patients. They are very susceptible to skin infections like that.

There are very low side effects from the Keytruda. Look, if he breaks his leg he can have surgery on that, but no more surgery on his head and neck. You would think he would be dead and buried by now. Based on my last operation on him a few days before Thanksgiving a few years ago, I knew I was leaving tumor behind at the skull base. Subsequent imaging showed erosion of that bone. That is no good. Keytruda killed that lesion, the aggressive cancerous tumor. The immunotherapy has kept him alive.

I've had numerous patients with squamous cell carcinoma. In general it is uncommon. I just had operated on a guy yesterday that was very similar to what I did on Richard. There are more and more people who are getting life ending skin cancers, which can be attributed to a number of things. First of all, cancer is a disease of old age. While a ten year old kid can get a cancer, it is unusual for kids to get solid tumor cancers. As we get older our immune systems—the T-cells that we count on—do not work as well. Patients are living longer and if you keep any biological thing alive long enough it will develop a neoplasm or malignancy. Also, more people today are immune-compromised from various drugs, transplants, etc.

Most cancers are a multi-hit phenomenon. Someone might say: "What do you mean I'm going to get cancer from smoking? My aunt smoked until she was ninety and never got cancer." She's lucky. But there's usually a number of things that come together to cause you to get a malignancy. Sunlight is increasingly recognized as something we can control as a white skinned person. But Richard's damage was not done last week, it was done forty years ago. It is accumulated damage. Sunlight causes certain chromosomal issues that over decades become cumulative. Then we add age, medications—all those things come together.

There are many immuno-compromised people. You see things advertised on TV for rheumatoid arthritis, inflammatory bowel disease, all these things. These all effect the immune system. It is a known cause. It is played down because they (drug companies) are making billions on this stuff.

I see people from all parts of the world who have been referred to me by other surgeons or other family members that I have treated. I do a fair amount of travel to Europe, the Middle East, North Africa to see patients and follow up on them. Most of it is from referral. If people like something about you, they tell other people about you. The truth is you have to like your patients and be able to bond with them. Any surgeon is going to have patients come to him. You can be a terrific surgeon but have a terrible bedside manner. People like Richard and others who have bonded to me, it isn't because I do their surgeries—it is because they like me as a person and I like them very much. I get emotional with them. I personally am not special. I do have experience treating patients that a lot of other people do not want to treat. I am well trained to do it. But a lot of surgeons, particularly cancer surgeons, may come off as aloof with patients. When you are dealing with a person whose life may end during the course of our treatment, if they feel you truly care about them, that becomes a special bond.

I had dinner with Richard Colton the night before his first big surgery. That was the first time I met him. He came up with Steve Metzinger's wife, Rebecca. Since then he and I have gone to dinner a number of times whenever he comes to Baltimore.

I'll be seeing him again in Baltimore in a few weeks. As my patient he will continue to see me twice a year. He will have his imaging before I see him, and then we'll talk about it. We have definitely extended his life and more importantly the quality of his life. He has no pain right now. But the nerves on the left side of his face are gone, similar to someone who had a stroke. He has a great spirit. I have seen him when he was down and in terrible pain and I would probably have been a lot worse. He isn't married, he doesn't have kids, but he has surrounded himself with a great support structure. The guy is beloved in New Orleans. I went to his birthday party. He has a nurse that they've sort of adopted each other. He has a cousin who comes with him all the time. He has a good friend who was a New Orleans Judge who often travels with him. He does have a very unique life. His home is like an art gallery. I just never want him to be lonely in his situation. I think I have more time alone than he does. He always has people around him.

He has a small life. He goes to doctor visits. He goes to the same place for lunch every day. I have gone to lunch with him. It is a greasy spoon place in New Orleans, but he likes it.

He goes with a few of his friends. His friend the Judge gets the same breakfast and lunch every day. He has the same breakfast at home: one banana and ten berries. I have gone to lunch with Richard at this place, Joey K's. It is two blocks from his house. Other than that I don't know what he does.

I wish I would have seen him ten years ago. I don't fully know what happened along the way. I don't really know if I could have turned it around.

* * *

Dr. William Sharfman
Interviewed April 27, 2018
Oncologist

I first met Mr. Colton in February of 2017. He had his first squamous cell cancer in 2012. I think he first came to Tufaro in 2014. I had no involvement until 2017 when Tufaro sent him to me. So when I first met him in 2017 he had been in radiation, and had the first operation for removal in 2014, then another in December of 2015. Then he had a third operation by Tufaro in November of 2016. When he had evidence of recurrence in the neck and cheek area and was in a lot of pain, Tufaro felt there was nothing more to be done surgically and he had the lifetime max of radiation. That is when I became involved.

It is a little confusing to some people as to what his diagnosis was. Head and Neck Squamous Cell Cancer is a more common thing. What Mr. Colton had is Squamous Cell cancer of the skin that metastasized to his neck and jaw bone on the left side of his face. That is interesting because skin squamous cancer is very common. There is a small operation called The Mohs Procedure where the surgeon cuts it out and that is the end of it. That is what happens in ninety-nine percent of the cases. It is unusual that his cancer progressed the way it has.

The first site of his skin cancer was on his left cheek. I wasn't there in the beginning, but that is how it started. As a Medical Oncologist my job is to find some type of intravenous or oral systemic therapy to try and get a disease in remission. At one time it would have been chemo therapy because there is no approved medical therapy for recurrent squamous cell skin cancer. There have never been enough patients to do studies. I guess it is technically an orphan disease. At least at Hopkins we are seeing a lot more of these patients. I am not sure why exactly that we are seeing a lot more, but it is still rare.

I am very involved in immunotherapy. Immunotherapy is therapy that turns on the immune system to recognize the cancer and eradicate it. My focus is melanoma and there have been great advances in immunotherapy of melanoma. As it turned out, there were reasons to believe that metastatic squamous cell of the skin would respond to immunotherapy.

This is something that I and many others thought was the way to treat cancer. I never thought that chemotherapy was going to be the answer. It makes more sense to eradicate a tumor by turning on the immune system. It is a more natural way of fighting cancer.

Starting about seven years ago, two new immunotherapy drugs became available. They are in this category we call "check point inhibitors." We all have in our immune system normal brakes that prevent the immune system from going overboard. If we didn't have these brakes in our immune system we'd all get Lupus or something. So the brakes are there for a reason. But these breaks are there to prevent the previous immune therapies from working. Immunotherapy works by turning off brakes in the immune system.

The first drug was called Yervoy, the generic is Ipilimumab. The second one is Nivolumab.

The other one is Pembro. So the two big breakthroughs were Pembro and Nivo. Pembro and Nivo, are drugs that we call PD1 inhibitors. These have been the big breakthroughs in immunotherapy for cancer in the last five years. Not for any kind of cancer but they do work on many kinds.

The first breakthroughs were for skin cancer and particularly in melanoma.

It was just becoming evident that it could work for the tumors in aggressive head and neck cancer. There were several anecdotal reports of these drugs working in Mr. Colton's type of cancer.

There are clinical trials going on now but at the time there was no data to collect from a clinical trial for this kind of cancer. Nonetheless, I thought this was his best shot. In his case I was able to petition Merck's drug, Keytruda, for Mr. Colton to use. It is not FDA approved but we got the company to let us test it on him. The formulation of the drug we chose was an every three week drug instead of an every two week drug because he had to come all the way from New Orleans to get it. We discussed it and he was game. We got the drug from the company, didn't have to worry about insurance approval—these are obviously extremely expensive—and we started on it.

He had his first dose of drug on February 17th, 2017 and his second dose March 14th. He had no particular side effects. One thing about these drugs—most patients don't get side effects. By the time he came in for the second dose of the treatment three weeks after the first his pain, which had been severe, started to ease up. We all thought that was remarkable.

The pain was in his jaw and neck area where the tumors had recurred. By the time he came back three weeks later, the pain had eased up significantly.

Every three weeks he gets another dose. It has been great. The pain is permanently gone and his CT scan is showing the tumors have shrunk dramatically. Cancer and treatment-wise he has done beautifully. But at one point he ran into some other health issues. He had a stroke, pneumonia twice. It was pretty severe pneumonia and he was hospitalized. I think these are all unrelated to the cancer or the immunotherapy. But he has been off treatment for two months or so because of all of that.

His last dose of treatment was January 10th. The pain did not come back. One of the things about these therapies is that sometimes, even when you stop them, they keep working. Even though he hasn't had a treatment since January, I think it is still working and helping him. So far there has been no recurrence of the cancer. We do a CAT scan quarterly to check.

Mr. Colton is a remarkable man, great spirit, nice man. He is very appreciative of everything that is done for him. He is a very unique guy; he comes with a whole entourage. He comes with his artist, a nurse, and his assistant. They are all very lovely people. With all the surgeries he has been through, it has been rough but he has a remarkable spirit and he pushes through. Even with these pneumonias and things he is pushing ahead.

We don't really know when to stop. In the initial immunotherapy trials the patients got treatment for two years, then they stopped and were monitored. I am using that as sort of a guideline and we will treat for two years these patients if they are benefitting from it. That would be my goal with Mr. Colton.

He isn't going to be penalized for missing treatment, we would try and get through a two-year period from whenever we started. Whether that is correct or not is not something we really know right now. Up until recently his prognosis would have been pretty guarded. He may not even have been alive now. With these newer immunotherapies some patients are going into remissions that are very long lasting. But there is no long term data with squamous cell skin cancer and these newer therapies. I can tell you in melanoma, which is mostly what I do, that we are putting about forty plus percent of people with metastatic melanoma into years of remissions. It is quite remarkable. For this exact disease I probably have like six or seven patients.

With squamous cell of the skin clearly sun exposure is a big part of it. I think we see a lot of these more aggressive squamous cells in men that are fair skin and have a lot of sun exposure. The combination of the sun and the fair skin is probably the most contributory. Why Richard's was so aggressive and wasn't controlled by surgery, we don't really know.

Some aggressive squamous skin cells patients have diminished immune cells. Like they have a lung transplant or they have ulcerative colitis and are on immunosuppressive drugs and then they get these aggressive squamous cells. That is a theme they are on some kind of therapy. But there are also patients who don't have that going on. They just seem to be fair skinned people with sun exposure. I don't know that we know there is a hereditary element with these aggressive cells on the skin.

Staying out of the sun is important. If you have fair skin, use sunscreens and go to the dermatologist to catch it early. He went to the doctor and was being monitored. Sometimes people get these aggressive skin cancers for reason we don't understand.

Right now all the patients with his exact cancer are doing well—except for one who is not responding. Since I started with Mr. Colton, there has been a clinical trial presented and published using a different company's PD1 inhibitor. So far the positive response rate is about fifty percent. Until recently we had like a twenty percent response rate, so a fifty percent response rate is pretty impressive. That is a small trial that needs more follow up. But it does look like the squamous cell of the skin does respond well to this kind of immunotherapy.

Given his being beyond radiation and more surgery, immuno was kind of the last real meaningful option. I think if he were to progress again there may be a different immunotherapy in the trial.

* * *

Dr. Benjamin Guidry

Interviewed January 14, 2019
Ophthalmologist

I'm a retina specialist. I'm basically where people get sent when the regular eye doctor is afraid someone is going blind. I see the hot and heavy stuff a lot.

Richard was referred to me approximately a year ago. His left eye had once had a vascular event—a small stroke—and it doesn't see much. He happened to have another issue in his right eye, his good eye, that required some injections to keep him doing as well as possible.

The left eye doesn't see much. It doesn't see the big "E." He can see you holding your fingers in front of his face but that's about it. I'm working on the good eye because he had a vascular event in that eye. He was seeing Dr. Rebecca Metzinger at the Tulane Ophthalmology Clinic at the time and I'm the retina specialist there, so when he had that event she sent him to me. That's when I met him.

I had to give him shots but you're still sticking a needle in an eye that someone's dependent on. The treatments I'm giving him are more to keep the vision as good as possible. The eye problem was big enough to reduce his vision for a little bit but he's recovered well.

The shot is what's called Avastin. It's a cancer drug that makes blood vessels go away. The cause is unclear. These little strokes in the eye can happen in anybody as long as you're of sufficient age. The leading causes: hypertension, diabetes. Cancer is kind of one of them because it can thicken the blood a little bit. As far as why it exactly happens, I'm not sure.

You wouldn't expect all this to happen from the Type Two diabetes he has in the absence of other diabetic issues. His is controlled enough to where it looks like it's separate.

Sometimes these things are gone in months or they take years. He looks like he's headed towards the tail end. The one I'm treating, his right eye, is a big chunk of what I do. It's always a little different when you know it's somebody's only eye. The stakes are a lot higher. If anything horrible happens to his right eye, he would need a lot of help.

I think he's a wonderful person. He has a beautiful sense of humor about everything. He seems to accept it very well—I guess the misfortunes he's gotten. He has a very beautiful persona. There are certain people that take it and make the most out of it, and it's just a beautiful thing to see.

He's the kind of person you enjoy helping. He's upbeat, very appreciative, and he's what ninety-nine percent of the doctors enjoy about their job. I'm glad he's doing well. I cross paths with him less and less and that's because he needs me less and less. He's the kind of person your life is richer for having them in.

***

Lincoln Collins

Interviewed June 13, 2018
Bloodstock, Consultant, Kern Thoroughbreds

I have been in the horse business a long time. I'm a bloodstock manager. What I do is I buy horses on people's behalf and sell them on people's behalf. So most of what I do is help people manage their racing stables—for example, someone like Dick who at one point needed professional management but didn't have enough horses to have a full-time manager. That is where I came in.

Richard Colton is one of the most fascinating human beings I have ever met, bar none. He is just remarkable. He has a very wide range of interests.

I guess I first met Dick twenty-five years ago. I have bought him a couple horses in England. He has had horses a very long time. Before I came around, he had a very good horse which I can't remember the name of right now but he won the New Orleans Handicap at the Fair Grounds. That was a great day for him to win a big race on his own doorstep. That is always exciting.

About 1995, Dick had a horse that we bought for him that died in trading here. That was sad. It was for no particular reason. So Dick called me up and he had a problem because the insurance company didn't want to pay the claim. Dick hadn't declared a previous surgery that the horse had had. It wasn't from any malice—he didn't know that you needed to do it, but it was one of the terms of the insurance policy. So I managed to get him paid. I knew the underwriters in London and was able to convince them that the last thing that Dick would be doing is killing a horse for insurance money. So he got paid. When things like that happen it can cost a lot of money and it was clear that he needed some professional advice, which is where I came in. I remember distinctly flying to New Orleans to meet with him.

He had already had a racing stable for a number of years. One of the most memorable days was when he had a horse called "Dernier Croise" who won a big race at Churchill Downs for a crowd of more than a hundred thousand people. The horse was ridden by a man named Gary Stevens. That was a great thrill. Dick and I have been all over the country together buying horses, or just going to see horses run. Every year we meet up in Saratoga and have a laugh and visit some of our old haunts.

Over the years his ability to judge horse flesh has improved. He would come to the sales and visit with the horses and get more comfortable around them.

The jockey is of great importance. For example, Gary Stevens was one of the top jockeys in the country and I doubt that horse would have won if he hadn't ridden him. When it really makes a difference is in those split-second decisions that make a difference between narrowly losing a race or winning a race narrowly. Very often it is the first time they have been on the horse. The better horses the top jockeys tend to ride regularly so they get to know the ins and outs of them. Certainly jockeys can develop an emotional relationship with a horse but it is the exception, not the rule.

Gary Stevens is actually the eldest jockey to ever win the Triple Crown at fifty-two. He has ridden for Dick in the past. By the way, Dick bought a horse called "Commander's Palace." I am sure there is a picture of the horse somewhere. Anyway, Commander's Palace, which I did not buy for him, was a head case. He did nothing in his stall except run around all day, which in horse terms is called being a stall walker. He was a pretty good horse but he could never be calm enough long enough to be a flat horse. So he actually got turned into a steeplechaser by a trainer we both know called Mickey Prager. The horse used to travel with his own special paddock so that he didn't run rampant all the time. A steeplechaser horse means when they run over jumps and race over jumps. He won the first race at

Saratoga one year. I can't remember the year. Consequently, Dick was the top owner in Saratoga for half an hour.

I am actually named after a racetrack in England. My family was very interested in it always. It is one of those things that happens. I originally wanted to be a race horse trainer.

I grew up on a house farm in England.

At any one time I probably deal with two hundred and fifty horses, but there have been thousands over the years. Though most of this game is constructed where eighty percent of it is random and you can control twenty percent. Even in the event of being able to control twenty percent that doesn't guarantee success. When you buy a yearling, you have no idea at all what it is going to be like in terms of racing ability. It is like picking out a ten year old that is going to run in the Olympic Games. The actual price you pay for the horse is a little bit like a lottery ticket. So Dick can ask what the yearling is worth and the question is really what it is going to take to buy it. Because once you have bought it, you are back to square one until it can prove that it can run.

You need luck to be successful in the horse business. Richard has had some very good horses. One horse, "Miss Lodi," we already knew she could run. Early in her career she won her first race. To cut a long story short, the top races are grade one, two and three. She won a stakes race, a grade three race... So she won a grade three race in Maryland, I believe. Then she was second or third on Kentucky Derby Day on grade one race. It wasn't the Kentucky Derby race but it was a grade one. When she retired from racing, we bred her and had a memorable sale. We thought she'd make a million and she sold for two million. That led Dick to make the marvelous remark, "Well, I still haven't sold a horse for a million dollars."

That was a big day. He has had several good winners all over the country. We had a lot of fun. But it is a frustrating game.

Just the nature of it… you rarely win—maybe twenty percent of the time. Eighty percent of the time you lose, even with horses, even at the top of their game, which is a disappointment.

If you are going to race, you are going to lose. The overwhelming likelihood is that racing horses is actually going to lose. Breeding horses, broadly speaking, is profitable. It is virtually impossible to make money racing horses. But if you buy a horse for a relatively lesser amount and sell that horse for two million, you are going to make money. But Dick did it because he loved the game as much as doing it with any thought of making money. What we tried to do was sell enough horses to be able to stay in the game.

At one point he had more horses than he wanted to have and sold off a great number.

That was shortly after I started working with him. That is one of the reasons Dick hired me to help him out. We sold off a bunch of horses trying to keep the better ones and get rid of the perennial losers both financially and in terms of success at the racetrack.

As for his illnesses and what he had been through in the last several years… I have had all the updates. It is amazing to me the fortitude with which Dick has come through the whole thing. I remember going back to him when the cancer had first started…it didn't seem to be all that serious initially and it got worse and worse. Obviously, I have known him for a long time so I have seen it eating away at him almost literally. But he has borne it amazingly well. They say that the attitude is half the battle. Most people would probably go backwards in terms of attitude when they have a problem like this. Dick has amazingly gone forward.

Dick has missed a few years in Saratoga obviously from illness but I will see him up there this year. Sadly, these days we don't see each other as much as we used to but we keep in touch. We have our annual reunion at Saratoga, get together and catch up.

He has a great sense of humor. We've done some amusingly contrarian things. He once bought a yearling in Saratoga for $770,000, which at the time was a big prize. There was a lot of publicity. Our haunt at Saratoga used to be the Saratoga diner. So rather than go to some fancy restaurant to celebrate once he bought the horse we went to the diner. That was the last thing that most race owners would do to celebrate, so we had agreed to do that. Joey K's was also a funny diner and we liked to go there.

I think Dick always enjoyed the farm and the backstretch. We would spend time here, then go to the Kentucky Derby. Being involved in the horse business is a whole lifestyle in itself. Being in it you make a lot of friends from all walks of life. There was an old guy who used to be the night watchman in Tom Amoss' barn; that was Dick's trainer. Dick was always friendly with him and I think they are in touch now. So here is this rich New Orleans man who is friends with this night watchman in the barn. Dick has always been like that. There is no snobbishness at all. He is one of the most kind-hearted people I have ever met.

* * *

Barton Jahncke

Interviewed November 28, 2018
Former VP for Lykes Bros. Steamship Co; Sailor
and Olympic champion

I went to work for Lykes Steamship Company. His father was an executive, but I first met Dick when I got out of Tulane in I think 1961. When I joined Lykes Brothers in a training program Dick was young. I would see his father in the New York office and so forth. Then I got to know Dick pretty well. I always liked him because he was smart and sensitive. He was painfully honest in a crazy industry and had good taste. He was generous with his time and resources and just a fine guy. He wasn't a member of the family but he and his siblings had a nice share of the company stock. His father was a Colton.

Dick was a free thinker. He would try new things. He was in marketing. He was good at it. He ended up being the Senior Vice President of Marketing. I was Vice President of Corporate Accounts. I had ninety accounts that I took care of worldwide. If we had any dealings with let's say Dupont, then everyone who worked for the company worked for me when we worked for Dupont, including the Chairman of the Board. That was in my job description.

One day I had this unbelievable stroke of luck when they were trying to figure out what they were going to do with Dick. I asked what they were talking about, and they trusted me, so I said I wanted him to join my group. I said he would be a real asset in what I was doing. Dick is a thinker. You don't have to tell him anything twice. He has a great memory, impeccable manner, great communicator, and he is the kind of guy I would take anywhere in the world and be proud of.

So we set up our shop on the twenty-second floor of the Lykes building. It was great. We had a wonderful gal, Linda, who worked for both of us. Dick and I had our own little enclave back there and we would commiserate. My door was open to him at all times and his door was open to me at all times. We both traveled a lot. If I was overseas and ran into something and needed quick guidance, I would pick up the phone and call Dick. He was a joy to work with. He was an associate, we were partners. He was a fine guy and I had great kids that he liked. He never had any children but he has had many kids who benefitted from a relationship with him. He is a fascinating guy. I've been a part of the whole horse thing and I don't know anything about horses. But he will take me to the track every so often. I was fascinated watching him and the jockeys and trainers. He was wonderful to my children and my first wife. He has also met my second wife of twenty years. He appreciates things. He shares his knowledge, his wealth. He is a generous, giving guy. You can't help but like him.

I think he got jerked around. He was a lot smarter than some of the other bulbs on the tree. Dick had patience but you could tell when he was beginning to get a little impatient. I don't think he would ever do anything to hurt anyone in a corporate battle. But he is a tough businessman. He knew how to stand his ground and was aggressive. Sometimes when you have a lot of family it is a difficult situation. I grew up in a family like that and never wanted to work for them. I think he had the potential and tools, he just got skipped over. But there were other things that stimulated him. He could look at himself every day and know he did a good job for Lykes.

I was in close proximity when he had his breakdown and fainted. I knew he was very depressed. What I tried to do was not let anyone lean on him. Let's put it this way, if someone wanted a piece of him, they had to get all of me. So I would tell Dick to take a break, just let me know and go home and rest if you need. I said to just stay in touch and if someone asked I would cover him. There was a time when I was really worried about him. I witnessed anxiety and depression. I guess everyone has that at times when your life gets a little out of balance. He had other things that stimulated him. You can't just look at Dick in one way: there are many chapters and colors in his rainbow. He is like fine linen, you know it when you see it.

With Dick Colton, he would always be in the ditch with me. A lot of people would run for the hills, not Dick. I had times when I was so frustrated trying to get something done and he would look at me and say, "Get a sailboat for the weekend."

That is another thing. I was very lucky that we had a Chairman of the Board who kind of said we should go win the gold medal. Now the President, Joe Lykes, didn't want me on the payroll and never did. So when the Chairman said to go win, something I had been dreaming of my whole life….he knew I was doing this for my dad and myself. Dick was fascinated with the effort and contributed financially and stuff like that. We were very fortunate.

He is a wonderful guy. There were times when I knew that Dick was down in the dumps. I told him one time to not look back because no one was gaining on him. He was holding his own. I love the guy. We've had a lot of fun and kidding and stuff in our lives.

Every time I see Dick we talk sports. He always asks about my kids. My son was a pretty good athlete and my daughter was a Ford model in New York. She did very well, went to NYU. Dick adored her. I think she is getting ready to change. She's been in a top job at Vanity Fair. She was the Executive Director of fashion and design. They are restructuring the whole company. She has a little girl and a great husband. We go up and spend time in the Hamptons with them.

The last time I saw Dick was in June. In fact, I was at the house and then we had lunch at Joey K's.

If someone asked me to sum Dick Colton up in twenty words or less, I would say he is a gentleman, a closet scholar. He keeps well read. He is multi-faceted, has a great sense of fair play, I think he is also a guy that when the going gets tough he will be there doing his share to make sure you succeed.

I know his battle with cancer has been extremely exhausting and somewhat experimental in some areas. He was looking really bad there for awhile and I told him that. I said he needed to get out in the sun and he just looked at me and said "I needed to see it from the other side." So he still has a great sense of humor. But it has been devastating for him. He is a guy that likes to be self-sustaining. He is proud and independent and now he has nurses helping him. I'm in awe, My God he is hanging in there.

He puts his money where his mouth is. He has a great sense of knowing when someone needs a little help or assistance. He has a group of friends that he has helped a lot. He brings good to their lives, whether just a calm sit down over a bowl of soup or a quiet contribution of finances. He does some wonderful things. He has done things very quietly, without putting his name on them.

There was a time when he had some kind of spiritual reawakening. I noticed he became more serene in life. I can just say we had a good time working together and now, long after, we both continue to value our relationship.

***

Dr. Erin Luft Katz

Interviewed September 11, 2019
General Dentistry

I first met Mr. Colton in 2014 when he became my patient. I have also been in a few of his cancer surgeries. He does have some dental challenges now. There was one tooth that had been causing him pain. We basically adjusted it enough to where it's not causing trauma to the tissue. With his muscle loss and the graft itself, he's not going to develop any more muscle tone or get rid of any of the neuropathy that's there. A lot of the sensation that he has is nerve pain, almost like phantom pain or neuropathy from his graft.

Although it feels like it, the pain was not because of some tooth cutting into his cheek. He is missing posterior teeth and the cheek kind of collapses onto that edge where his dentition starts. Because he's missing the posterior teeth, and because of the lack of muscle tone in the graft, the most we can really do is we soften it so there's not constant trauma. Aside from putting something there to kind of pull the cheek out, there's really no option because he's at risk for other issues in terms of damaging the graft that he had on his resection. As you know, he's not a candidate for implants or anything like that.

We know he can't have any more x-rays or radiation of any sort, more chemo or more surgery. Our biggest concern with him is maintaining what he has now, knowing that if he has a tooth that needs to be extracted it's not a simple procedure for him. He's going to have to undergo this in a hospital-type setting due to all the procedures and radiation he had. It changes his quality of life. Granted he has life, and that in itself is a miracle, but the lasting effects of the radiation and surgeries he's had have definitely made maintaining his teeth a very complex and not easy task.

He does have many teeth left. He had two implants placed prior to his diagnosis with cancer and those are healthy. He has about 75% of his lower dentition. The biggest thing for him is preventing any decay and keeping him comfortable mainly from changes to his saliva, which could be long-lasting dry mouth from radiation. The part of his jaw that was resected included the removal of salivary glands. Not only does he have less saliva from surgery, he has less saliva from lasting effects of all this chemo and radiation. The medication he has to stay on for the rest of his life can have the effect of dry mouth. That not only changes the quantity of his saliva but it can also change the quantity or the pH, which could make him more susceptible to decay and make the saliva less lubricating for his tongue, his lips, and his cheek.

It can also change his ability to taste. Likewise, he might have certain foods he's more sensitive to. He may have lasting metallic taste or burning tongue sensation. All of that can be related back to things he's gone through in order to save his life.

We suggested he use a straw to drink because he has trouble swallowing and closing his mouth. Using a straw will help him to be able and willing to drink more. I think even maybe subconsciously he's drinking less because he has a problem with fluid falling out. But because of the changes to his saliva he needs to consume more water.

We see him every three months to maintain and make sure we're able to catch anything before it's problematic. Like I said, for him extracting a tooth would basically be a trip to the operating room, whereas with anybody else if you need a tooth pulled it's an office visit. In the hospital he might have to undergo treatment with a bariatric pressure tank to lower the risk of osteoporosis of the jaw. He's not a candidate for replacing teeth with an implant anymore and is at risk with anything like a partial or removable bridge causing traumatic ulcers that may never heal or cause him more problems.

I will say as a person he's very straightforward and he's obviously had a lot of life experiences, having gone through what he's gone through. He's willing to put whatever he wants to say out there. He once told me as he was sitting in the third floor of my office looking out that I needed to call someone to trim the trees. I said I would get right on that. He's a difficult patient not because of personality but because of everything he's gone through. He's understandably fearful. It's not easy for him to open his mouth. It's not easy for us to put a lot of things in there.

I've had patients with a history of head and neck radiation or jaw resection but not as severe as him. The fact that he's alive is amazing. We see him every three months. His dental hygiene is much improved—more recently than I had ever seen in the past. His nurses help him a lot in this regard. I'm sure that when you're in pain it's difficult to make dental hygiene a priority. You probably just want to go to bed and not worry about brushing your teeth or rinsing out your mouth. He's now regularly using his Waterpik and the ultrasonic toothbrush we gave him. He has to be meticulous with his oral hygiene because he's at higher risk for bacteria in his mouth, whether it's bacteria that cause decay or bacteria that causes periodontal disease. He's going to have an increase in both and an increase in complications for what's going to arise from those bacteria.

It's a price you pay for staying alive in an extreme situation like his where Stage Four squamous cell skin cancer has ravaged his head, neck, and jaw. He's a walking miracle and it's not easy. I don't know if I would have been able to get through an ordeal like this as courageously as he has.

* * *

Acknowledgments

Although this may be difficult at times, it is important for anyone who is going through a cancer journey, or has gone through one, to have someone there with them along the way to take notes, to remember dates, to do all the things that could someday be compiled into a book. I am most fortunate to have had more than one such remarkable helpers.

Traveling down a winding road in the course of my decade-long battle against a deadly form of cancer was definitely not a trip I took alone in any way. The remarkable physicians who treated me with state-of-the-art medical care, and even more, with real *care,* include doctors Anthony Tufaro, Charles Smith, Stephen Metzinger, Coller Ochsner, William Sharfman, and Benjamin Guidry.

How blessed am I as well with my equally capable and caring nurses, Susan Badeaux, RN; Kristine Maruri, RN; Judith Dodd, DNP; aides Elena Maruri and Angela McCleney, and my irreplaceable executive assistant, the aptly named Sherrie Soule.

Traveling back and forth to Johns Hopkins would have been far less comfortable without my Baltimore travel team: cousin John Carrere, who is my "Executive Vice President of Logistics," and, again, the wonderful, ever-vigilant Susan Badeaux.

Friends are jewels in the crown of life. For me, none are more so than Judge Dennis Waldron and his phenomenal sons, Matthew, Andrew, and James. They were and are always there when I need them most, and are the best pals I could have wished for. I also owe a debt of gratitude to my former business colleague and cherished friend Barton Jahncke.

Barton understood me; we had mutual respect, worked well together, and always had each other's back.

Family is forever. Sending much love to my younger sisters, Keenan, Kelsey, and Elizabeth Colton, for their support and for always working hard to maintain our close family ties. Love too, to my wonderful nieces and nephews: Keenan's son Sean and daughter Megan, and Elizabeth's daughter Ashley and son R.J. You have all been a source of pride and joy from the moment you were born. I also want to give a warm hug from afar to my beloved half-sister Ginny Paulson, whom I never see enough of and miss much.

Horse sense has sometimes eluded me, and I owe a debt of gratitude to bloodstock expert and advisor in the horse business, Lincoln Collins, for always guiding me in the right direction when buying, selling or breeding those beautiful creatures. Of course it all started with John Carrere's old college roommate Sam Hinkle, and Sam's mother, Mrs. Jane Collins Hinkle, on her thoroughbred horse farm in Shelbyville Kentucky. I miss both Sam and Jane, as they have both passed away this year. They will always be in my heart.

Thank you Monica Thompson, for always making my pre-surgery to Dr. Tufaro so pleasant. I am also indebted to my own office manager Juliet DiStefano! I want to thank, too, my personal trainer, Betsy Becker Laborde, the former Assistant Athletic Director at Tulane, who keeps me moving and "in balance" several times a week. Way to go, Betsy!

Thank you, artist Terrance Osborne, for your immense talents and the Richard Colton section in your popular art gallery. Speaking of fine artists, Taryn Möller Nicoll fills these pages—and my walls—with her enormous talents and abiding friendship. I heartily congratulate her on being appointed the new chief curator of the Frank C. Ortis Art Gallery & Exhibit Hall in Pembroke Pines, Florida.

Bronson Thayer's confidence in me has made me a better man. And my nurse Susan's father, James Sullivan Badeaux, who lost his valiant battle against heart disease in May 2019, inspired me at my lowest moments.

Jordan Selden, Sherrie's beautiful 21 year old daughter, went over the manuscript carefully with me, page by page, not once but twice. She was most patient and helpful.

My collaborator Judy Katz brought someone very special to the project: another amazing writer, Kai Flanders. They say behind every man is a good woman. Kai's woman, Mickey Suzuki, is beautiful and accomplished—one of a kind. Thank you, Mickey, for being so understanding of the time Kai spent working with Judy and me—both from your home in Los Angeles, to several trips he and Judy took so that we could work together here in The Big Easy—on a project which was big, but not so easy!

I want to send a warm note of gratitude to the talented and meticulous Bev Nicholls, who was my CPA for many years, and likewise express my appreciation for her husband, Ray Nicholls, also a good friend, who sadly passed recently. It is always painful to lose good friends.

I can't close out these acknowledgments without thanking my spiritual advisor Father Val McInnes, whom I and the world lost in November 2011. I also want to thank our dear mutual friend, Jackie Sullivan, who was so good to Father Val, and to me, for so many wonderful years we had together.

I also want to acknowledge a most remarkable woman, Leah Chase, chef, author, television personality and owner of the famed New Orleans restaurant, Dooky Chase. Beloved by all, Leah will be sorely missed by all, most especially me.

Last but certainly not least, I want to acknowledge Martin and Jessica Dougherty, my dear friends, who quoted this sage Irish proverb to me: "It is in the shelter of each other that people live." That is certainly true of my cancer journey. I have also tried my best to provide a bit of "shelter" for others whenever and wherever I could. But, unquestionably, without this medical team, and these friends and family, I would not be here to tell you my story.

I surely have neglected to name many others who have likewise played an important part in my life, whether in a short role or one that spanned years. Forgive the omission, and know that your contribution was deeply appreciated. We are all in this life together, and I hope I have graced your life as well in some small measure.

My love to one and all.

Richard Colton

About the Author

Richard C. Colton Jr. is a retired business executive and a well-known and much-loved New Orleans philanthropist and patron of the arts. His fascinating life has had many acts, the most recent of which is his decade-long battle with a rare and deadly form of cancer. It called for a miracle, received one, and left him spiritually changed. His memoir, *No More. No Less: An Artful Cancer Journey. A Remarkable Community. A Rediscovered Purpose (New Voices Press, November, 2019)*, chronicles that dramatic and ultimately triumphant journey. His website is richardcolton.com

The author in his element, hosting frequent fundraisers in his home. The chef, Tommy Finch, was originally discovered in Commander's Place. Now practicing his culinary skills in Brooklyn, NY, he always graciously returns to cater parties for me.

About Judy Katz

Judy Katz is a book collaborator, ghostwriter, publisher and marketer. She has helped develop storylines for prospective authors, and has successfully completed, published and publicized 45 books so far.

After graduating from UC Berkeley, where she had her own column, "Meaning's Edge," on the *Daily Californian* for all four years, she wrote for a medical ad agency and two McGraw-Hill Magazines before becoming PR Director for Madison Square Garden, and the New York March of Dimes, and Director of Special Projects for the National MS Society.

Entrepreneurial, Judy then established and ran her own PR firm, Katz Creative, Inc., until 2005, when she found her true passion: helping people become successful authors. Judy also has a publishing arm, New Voices Press, and along with self-publishing helps promote her authors' books to serve them as "the ultimate marketing and reputation-building tool."

Judy is a proud member of the Author's Guild, PEN America, MENSA, and many other prestigious professional and networking organizations. Her website is katzcreativebooksandmedia.com. She can also be found on LinkedIn and Facebook.

Judy can be reached at 212-580-8833
or jkatzcreative@gmail.com.

www.ingramcontent.com/pod-product-compliance
Lightning Source LLC
Chambersburg PA
CBHW040324300426
44112CB00021B/2866